THEATER CAREERS

THEATER CAREERS
A Realistic Guide

Tim Donahue and Jim Patterson

The University of South Carolina Press

© 2012 University of South Carolina

Published by the University of South Carolina Press
Columbia, South Carolina 29208

www.sc.edu/uscpress

Manufactured in the United States of America

21 20 19 18 17 16 15 14 13 12   10 9 8 7 6 5 4 3 2 1

Library of Congress Cataloging-in-Publication Data
Donahue, Tim, 1952–
  Theater careers : a realistic guide / Tim Donahue and Jim Patterson.
    p. cm.
  Includes bibliographical references and index.
  ISBN 978-1-61117-080-1 (cloth : alk. paper) — ISBN 978-1-61117-081-8 (pbk : alk. paper)
  1. Theater—Vocational guidance—United States. 2. Acting—Vocational guidance—United
States. I. Patterson, Jim (Jim Aris) II. Title.
  PN2074.D66 2012
  792.02'3—dc23
                                    2012008081

CONTENTS

Introduction

If you are in one of the five groups identified here, *Theater Careers* was written especially for you:

High school students who want a career in theater

High school students contemplating further training in theater

Guidance counselors who need better understanding of the facts about careers in theater in order to help students

College students looking for the facts before they leap into a theater career or graduate training after graduation

Parents of high school or college students determined to forge a theater career

There are many books offering *advice* for aspiring theater folk, mostly actors: *how to manage your career, how to find an agent, how to audition, how to be a better actor, how to etc., etc.* These books are full of *opinions*—some worthwhile, some not. *Theater Careers* is clearly different. Here are the facts and not just for aspiring actors. *Theater Careers* presents the full spectrum of theater careers:

What kind of theater jobs are out there? And where?

How much do they pay?

What training and experience are required to land those jobs?

What sort of higher education prepares the student for those careers?

What are some real examples of people, mostly actors, who changed their career paths but remained in theater?

How can you stay current on theater jobs?

Theater Careers is concise, clear, and current. The facts you need to know to make informed decisions about a career in theater are here.

Different Approaches to the Text

The way to use this book is up to you. Chapter 1, for example, is mostly a list of real theater job descriptions. After reading the introductory paragraphs, you might want to skim the job descriptions. Read or skim other chapters, and then perhaps file *Theater Careers* away for future readings, then return to it again as a reference source. It's up to you!

For any chapters you skip or skim, be sure to read the closing section titled "Beyond the Facts." If you find the inferences and opinions offered in the "Beyond the Facts" sections surprising or unbelievable, you probably need to read the chapter to discover how the inferences and opinions are backed up by the facts. Like any writers, we hope you'll read the whole book.

This book, then, is a dense collection of facts. We believe that high school seniors and college undergraduates are prepared—having been educated and having matured—to absorb the facts and consider them in decision making. So are parents and guidance counselors.

What It Takes

Some students, whether they are in university or in middle and high school, develop the goal—the urge, the *compulsion*—to work in theater. It's easy to see why. In community theater and school productions, they find something special that really moves them. Whether actor, scene painter, flyman, or some other position in a production, members of a theater company bond intensely during the lead-up to opening night. The rehearsal and technical run-throughs make the theater a welcoming place to collaborate. The goal is clear: to perform the script. The opening date is set. Together the company succeeds or fails. The camaraderie is intoxicating.

Applause when the curtain rises to reveal the set is thrilling. Achieving a theatrical transformation with setting, lights, and costumes is a group accomplishment. Eliciting laughter is rich feedback. Accepting the title of "artist" enhances self-esteem. And theater people are usually fun to be with. They may laugh more easily than most people. They're not ashamed to show that they feel deeply. They share with others in the company because the success of one person is the success of all. A few young people drawn to theater may have felt like outsiders in their schools and communities; in a theater company, they have a gang to hang with. Groups making theater have a sense of creating something, belonging to a special crowd.

The good news is that much of the positive experience of company members in educational or amateur theater is also available in the professional theater. Theater folk can be funny, committed, emotionally available, and sometimes a little quirky. As in any workplace, however, one's fellow workers can sometimes be obstinate, self-involved, competitive, and unfair too. Theater people run the gamut. The bad news is that creating a career in theater that will supply enough money and security to live decently, have a family, and eventually retire with relative comfort is difficult for the vast majority of those who try. That a successful theater career is hard to obtain is the common wisdom, and the facts collected here for the most part confirm that truism.

But some people do succeed at a career in theater. If we thought that no one should work in theater, we would have no reason to write *Theater Careers*. As people who love theater, we absolutely want to see the next generation of theater artists develop and display its talents and insights.

In the age of the Internet and Google, facts should be easy to obtain. They are available, here and there, bit by bit. However, in this book, for the first time, the available facts from government and other resources for working in the professional theater have been collected in one place and organized. The result reveals patterns and provokes inferences that are revealing and compelling for aspiring students, parents, and career guidance professionals.

Those who have a theater career as their life goal should know what it may be like, but few books, teachers, or counselors tell the whole story or present a wide range of hard facts. *Theater Careers* offers a realistic depiction of what awaits that average person seeking a career in theater, whether as a designer, technical support person, stage manager, actor, director, etc.

An Important Bias

Theater Careers espouses higher education and lifelong learning. Get all the education you can use. Learning doesn't stop when schooling stops. Pursue learning honestly and be prepared to be changed by what you learn. Know that everyone needs to make money, yes, but everyone also needs a deep experience of the meaning of one's life story, era, and culture that lifelong learning provides. Other than this exhortation to learn, this book offers little advice. Each chapter concludes with a "Beyond the Facts" section that outlines inferences from the facts the chapter presents. We also offer in these brief chapter conclusions some limited, clearly identified opinions based on the content of the chapter. However, the bulk of *Theater Careers* is just the facts.

Goals

This book is devoted to presenting solid, baseline information about the choices and chances awaiting a high school graduate or undergraduate theater major seeking a career in theater. There are no prerequisites for reading *Theater Careers*. It defines terms—for example, clarifying the differences among the various degree programs represented by acronyms such as B.A., M.A., B.F.A., M.F.A., A.A., and others. It assumes the reader needs to know these and other basics.

In theater or elsewhere, no career a young person plans is a slam dunk. Every journey is risky. Schooling, early employment, strategic choices for second and subsequent employers or for self-employment, and so on are all fraught with risk. Considering employment averages for theater alone tells a distorted picture of the risks unique to theater. Thus *Theater Careers* compares average theater graduate salaries with a few other B.A. areas of study.

Even if you decide that a career in theater is not for you, there are many ways to be involved in theater as a hobbyist, financial supporter or investor, or audience member. In a brief afterword, these alternatives are presented.

Training in many theater skills can also prepare one for jobs elsewhere and in other media. Without a doubt some actors work on stage, on television, and in film. Less often directors work on stage and in film. Designers work in all media and set and lighting designers are increasingly working in commercial design for restaurants, bars, stores, and even religious buildings. A trained tailor or seamstress can work most anywhere. So can a good carpenter. That being said, *Theater Careers* covers only the live theater.

Talent

Webster's Dictionary defines *talent* as "any natural aptitude or skill." Talent reflects hard-wiring, a genetic inheritance, which is different from knowledge or training. Talent is at least in part instinctive. There are degrees of talent as there are degrees of anything. Another perspective is that talent creates an inequality in ability that affects how much different people benefit from training. Talent is usually discussed in opposition to hard work, grit, or determination, but grit in practicing a talent, an unrelenting focus on practice and improvement, can be the difference between remaining a talented amateur and maturing into a professional. You can be very talented but unwilling to work, psychologically inflexible, and so on, and thus never be very good. You can be talented and never have fame or financial success, both of which require an element of luck. You can have a minor talent, understand it, nurse it, grow it, and have a rewarding career. Talent is innate but wasted on people who are inert.

Who is talented enough to succeed in theater? *No one knows.* There are no standardized tests for theatrical talent. You must have the necessary talent to have a meaningful career in most theater fields, but success as a theater professional requires *more* than talent. It requires an adventurous spirit, perseverance, resilience, hard work, the ability to live with ambiguity and accept failure, great social skills, training, and *luck.* Working hard is also necessary but that quality alone won't guarantee a successful theater career. Perhaps the talented and prolific playwright David Lindsay-Abaire, a writer of successful stage plays and film scripts, summarized the situation best: "We have this myth that if you work hard, you can accomplish anything. It's not a very American thing to say, but I don't think that's true. It's true for a lot of people, but you need other things to succeed. You need luck, you need opportunity, and you need the life skills to recognize what an opportunity is." We endorse Mr. Lindsay-Abaire's observation.

One final observation: *Theater Careers* is specific about the *average experience* of people seeking a career in theater. By absorbing this information, young people, their counselors, and their parents will be better prepared to judge whether a career in theater is a worthy goal, whatever the young person's talent.

CHAPTER 1

The Many Jobs in Professional Theater

Facts show that there are hundreds of different jobs available in the commercial and not-for-profit (NFP) theaters. It takes many kinds of workers to mount a production: playwrights, directors, actors, designers, managerial staff, and technical hands. Few people outside of the professional theater know what a great number of workers and what a variety of jobs it takes to put on a show or support an NFP theater. This fact is good news for young people eager to make a career in professional theater.

A quick survey of only five productions playing in New York City during one recent season, using issues of *Playbill* and programs for evidence, found remarkable differences in the number of positions listed in the credits for shows. The average number of credited workers on a show was just fewer than 150 in this small, unrepresentative sample. In the end it doesn't matter if there is one actor or twenty-three on stage. The number of actors has little-to-no relationship with the number of workers needed to put on a show. See table 1.

Table 1: Selected Numbers of Credits in New York City Professional Theater Productions

Theater Type	Producing Organization	Number of Actors	Number of Workers Listed in Program Credits
Broadway	Commercial	2	120
Broadway	Not-for-Profit	1	166
Broadway	Commercial	20	208
Off-Broadway	Commercial	23	84
Off-Broadway	Not-for-Profit	5	169

Not all workers on a show, however, are credited in the program and thus are not included in the numbers in table 1. Most lower level and entry-level positions, such as stitcher, carpenter, deck crew, rigging crew, and so on are not listed in professional theater programs, In sum there are more workers on each of the productions detailed in table 1 than the program credits. Generally, not-for-profit theaters credit more people in their programs than do commercial theaters. In fact the difference between NFP and commercial theaters are important for job seekers to know.

Two Business Structures of Professional Theater

There are two main structures, commercial and not-for-profit, for professional theater in the United States. With few exceptions commercial theater is limited to much of Broadway and touring and some of off-Broadway.* Practically all other professional theater in the United States is not-for-profit. This includes virtually all regional theaters, that is, the professional theaters outside of New York City. The differences between the commercial and not-for-profit forms of theater are important facts to understand when considering what kinds of jobs are available in theater.

Commercial Theater

The commercial theater is usually constructed as a limited liability partnership or limited liability company that produces a single show on Broadway or off-Broadway and has rights to certain subsequent earnings of the script if the production is successful. The partnership generally lasts for eighteen years after the show opening. In the partnership there is a managing partner, traditionally called the producer, who makes all decisions and usually does not invest money in the show. The rest of the partners invest or raise money but have no say in running the show. Successful producers run offices and have staff on hand to carry out some functions for any shows they produce, but producers also hire consultants such as lawyers and insurance advisers, and they sometimes contract with key staff for specific shows, such as the general manager, whose duties are detailed later. Among their hires are the creative staff for an individual show, including director, designers, actors, and the like. Producers do not typically own the buildings in which their shows are presented. Instead they license theaters from the owner/operators or, for touring shows, enter into contracts with local venues and presenters. Thus some of the jobs associated with running the theater building are not filled by the producer but by the theater owner. Fig. 1 is an organizational chart for a fictional but typical commercial theater production.

---

* There are a couple of exceptions. One example, although involving fewer and fewer productions, is dinner theater, which is always organized as a for-profit venture. We estimate that fewer than three dozen dinner theaters operated in the United States in the early years of the twenty-first century, down from more than one hundred in the 1960s. Another exception might be the small number of commercial shows that "sit down" for long runs in Las Vegas hotel/casinos, but these can be regarded as extensions of commercial theater touring, almost always a commercial activity.

Commercial Theater
Example Organizational Chart

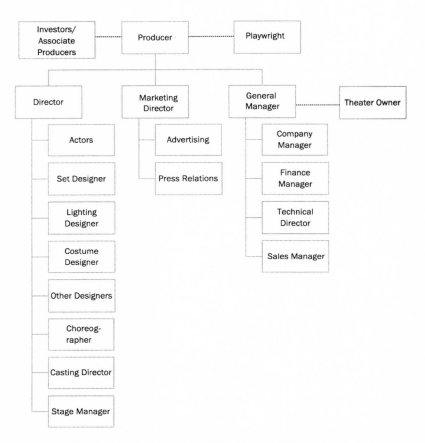

Fig. 1. This is a typical organization chart for a commercial theater production.
Solid lines show hiring and firing authority. Dotted lines indicate a collaborative relationship.
For example, the playwright is not an employee of the producer, hence the dotted line.

For completeness we should mention that some for-profit corporations have produced commercial shows on Broadway and in touring. The most notable and successful of recent years is the Disney Corporation, producer of *Beauty and the Beast, The Lion King, The Little Mermaid, Tarzan,* and other shows.

Not-for-Profit Theater

By contrast the not-for-profit theater is formed as a not-for-profit *corporation.* As a corporation, the NFP theater doesn't disband after producing a single show;

rather it hopes to last in perpetuity. A NFP theater is a 501(c)(3) corporation—an Internal Revenue Service–approved designation—that makes it exempt from many federal, state, and local taxes. Donations to 501(c)(3) corporations are tax-deductible for the donors.

Not-for-profit theaters list in their programs and playbills many organizational positions that either do not exist in the commercial theater or are not typically credited in the commercial theater. For example, NFP theaters have development departments (involving fund-raising, donation, and grant management), many have education departments, and most run their own theater buildings.

Beginning NFP theaters usually rent performance spaces, but successful theaters often wind up owning at least one theater space. Therefore an NFP theater typically employs a number of positions that the commercial producer does not, these being people needed to maintain and operate a building. One NFP theater for example, Steppenwolf in Chicago, owns and operates its several performance spaces *plus* a parking garage as part of its theater structures. In the commercial theater, the theater buildings are licensed by show producers, and building employees such as box office staff, ushers, and the like are hired by the theater and do not report to the producer. Fig. 2 is a typical example of an organizational chart for a not-for-profit theater group.

The NFP theater typically raises funds from individuals and groups, and in addition to that it also applies for and has to account for grants from governments and foundations. Donations and grants—called "unearned income"—are typically about 40 to 60 percent of a not-for-profit theater's budget. Some NFPs receive marketing support as donations in kind from local marketing or advertising agencies, but others have internal marketing departments. In many cases, a not-for-profit theater has educational programs for schoolchildren in the theater's community. All these activities require specialized staffing that is not generally needed by the professional theater. Many—but far from all—not-for-profit professional theaters give at least some effort to developing and presenting new plays, and this activity requires personnel with special skills, education, and experience. There is probably more variation in the employment practices of the not-for-profit theater than there is in the commercial theater. Note that within the NFP professional theaters, there is great variation in size and sophistication, and thus also in how many and what sort of positions that are employed. Among the largest of these organizations, that is, those with the most employees, three so-called super-NFPs in New York City produce in Broadway houses and are thus eligible for Tony Awards: Lincoln Center Theater, Manhattan Theatre Club, and Roundabout Theatre. There are also nationally known organizations such as the Guthrie Theater in Minneapolis, the Steppenwolf Theatre in Chicago, the Arena Stage in Washington, DC, and many others.

Not-for-Profit Theater
Example Organizational Chart

Fig. 2. A typical organizational chart for a NFP theater organization. In a NFP corporation, the board of directors manages the group for the public good; in doing so, it hires, evaluates, and fires if necessary, the artistic and managing directors.

Some important NFP festival theaters began as summer events but have grown to being six- and nine-month endeavors, such as the Oregon Shakespeare Festival and the Utah Shakespearean Festival. There are NFP historical pageants that play outdoors in the summer months, many of which began in the 1930s, including *Unto These Hills* in Cherokee, North Carolina, and *Tecumseh!,* in Chillicothe, Ohio. There are regional theaters that engage an acting company for an entire season and others that hire actors for a single show. Then there are many smaller companies that are important within their communities just as there are many start-ups that hope to become essential to the cultural life of their hometowns.

Professional Theater Job Descriptions

This chapter presents many of the most often occurring jobs. The job titles that follow were gathered from issues of *Playbill* and programs of commercial and NFP theaters. Job descriptions for the job titles were summarized by reviewing job offers posted in trade journals and on the Internet to discover typical job duties and requirements.

Theater jobs can be divided into six different general areas:

Managerial
Artistic
Technical/crew
Theater support
Education (within not-for-profit theaters that have education programs)
Consultants/services

This classification of jobs is not to comment on the value of the job or worker. All theater jobs contribute to the success of the commercial or NFP theater. Most any theater job is "artistic" to some extent, but the divisions used here clarify essential differences. Playwrights are saved to the end of this discussion because they are usually not employees of either the commercial or NFP theater.

Because training and evaluation of musicians and other musical jobs are a specialized activity quite separate from that of theater artists, *Theater Careers* does not consider those job titles and descriptions. However, in union theaters, dancers are members of Actor's Equity Association and choreographers are members of the Stage Directors and Choreographers Society, so they have been included here.

Few organizations would hire all the positions described here. Job duties differ greatly between organizations of different sizes. Outside of union requirements, employers have freedom in how they title jobs and how they assign responsibilities to employees, so these job descriptions should be considered general and typical. They are descriptive, not prescriptive. In sum these explanations of the positions are amalgams of job descriptions used by some NFP theaters and commercial producers, focusing on the essential duties.

In our research we have determined that NFP theaters with large budgets often have more highly developed and refined job descriptions than do smaller NFPs. One cause of this variation in sophistication of job descriptions may be greater job differentiation in a larger organization. When a group starts up, the founding artistic director and the board may find themselves doing whatever is necessary: painting scenery, cleaning toilets, ripping tickets, or the like. As the group grows with more staff, duties become more fully defined. A bigger organization has more at stake and becomes concerned about perpetuating the group and preserving it from risks, including those associated with litigation resulting from hiring and firing decisions. A small organization is unlikely to have a dedicated human resources department to prepare detailed job descriptions.

Differences in commercial and not-for-profit duties and/or job titles are described where relevant. The usual clichés of job descriptions, such as "and other duties as assigned" are omitted. Some of these positions might have subordinates with the titles "assistant," "associate," or the like, depending on the organization's size. Also left out are requirements to direct staff or work under the approval of some other position. Nearly every job description of any specificity we consulted in compiling this list mentioned the need for at least some level of computer skills. Every organization today, even theater, is reliant on e-mail and other electronic communications that require capability with a keyboard and the ability to read, comprehend, and write clear prose.

Management Jobs
Producer

The producer's job in the commercial theater is to create, organize, and direct the partnership that will stage one play or musical with the goal of making a profit for the investors in the production. To that end the producer chooses the material to be produced; attracts investors; hires legal counsel to draft partnership documents, options on the source material to be staged, and the like; hires a general manager who develops budgets and continues to oversee the details of project direction and decision-making; licenses a theater building for the run; hires the director and designers and is usually involved with casting at least the lead actors; and engages marketing and advertising staff to develop and implement a marketing strategy. For some musicals, the producer will identify source material in other media—novels, films, record albums—to be dramatized and then engage writers and composers to create a script. One producer defines the job as the "three Fs": find it (the script), fund it (secure investors), fill the seats (manage marketing).

For long-running productions, the producer may be involved in deciding whether brush-up rehearsals are needed, in casting replacements, with continued marketing and press relations, and in deciding when and how the show will tour in the United States and be staged in other countries. Most often the producer will produce at least the early road tours, but in some cases the producer will license some other entity to produce one or more tours.

Since the 1990s most commercial shows have had multiple producers. Typically one of the producers will be designated the lead producer with the power to make decisions for the show. The other producers will primarily be money raisers.

When not producing a specific show, a producer searches for material that is capable of being profitably produced, maintains relationships with past and potential investors, and identifies talent for future shows: writers, composers, directors, designers, actors. All this is done with the producer's main goal in sight: to create, organize, and direct a partnership for the profit-making commercial production of a play.

In the not-for-profit theater, the producer, executive producer, and associate producer have duties that are more comparable to those of the general manager in the commercial theater than the duties of a producer in the commercial theater.

The commercial producer is the owner-operator of a production, not an employee, and so is not represented by a union. Many are members of the Broadway League, a trade organization representing commercial theater owners and producers. The league negotiates contracts with theatrical labor unions, cosponsors the Tony Awards, and promotes the Broadway brand name. Off-Broadway commercial producers may belong to the League of Off-Broadway Theatres and Producers.

Many producers begin in other areas of theater, especially as general managers or as assistants in a producer's office. The Commercial Theater Institute (CTI), a project of the Broadway League and the Theatre Development Fund (TDF), presents workshops and seminars for those interested in learning about commercial theatrical production.

The producer is the business owner and receives no salary as such. When a show is running, the producer receives a set amount per week for "office expenses," and 2 or 3 percent of gross revenues. After recoupment—meaning return of the original investment to the investors out of a show's weekly profit—the producer shares in a percentage of the show's profit, up to 50 percent but more typically negotiated downward to as little as 15 percent. The producer, for example, may be forced to sacrifice some of his traditional half-share in profits in order to hire the star, director, choreographer, or designers that the producer judges are necessary to the show's success. Given the producer's share of profits and the control of touring and foreign productions, his or her return from a hit can be very large. Cameron Mackintosh, the British and international producer of *Cats, Les Misérables, Miss Saigon, The Phantom of the Opera*, and others, was estimated in spring 2010 to have a net worth of £650 million, approximately one billion U.S. dollars.

General Manager

In the not-for-profit theater, similar duties might be described as those of the head of production, production director, or producer.

A general manager handles the day-to-day business for a specific production that may include negotiating contracts; administering and supervising financial procedures including banking, preparing budgets, paying bills, and supervising ticket sales; and producing the weekly profit/loss statement in the commercial theater. The general manager is often the liaison between artistic personnel and producer, oversees the company manager, and often is a trouble-shooter. The general manager may cast replacement actors for small roles. As one commentator noted, the general manager in the commercial theater does whatever the producer doesn't want to do. The general manager usually has a staff and may manage more than one show at a time. General managers for Broadway shows often fulfill the same function for any touring productions. Some commercial producers have full-time staff who fulfill the general manager role for their own productions and may contract to manage other producers' productions.

In the commercial theater, the general manager receives a flat fee when contracted for a production plus a weekly fee beginning two weeks before the start of rehearsals and continuing through the run. Some general managers receive a percent of net profit. Terms are negotiated between the general manager and the producer and are variable. For a Broadway musical, the initial fee might be between $35,000 and $45,000, the weekly fee $4,500. The fee for a Broadway play might be about $30,000 with $3,500 weekly. In the not-for-profit theater, the general manager is typically a salaried employee of the corporation, and salaries vary greatly with the size of the not-for-profit's budget. There is no union for general managers, but general managers who began their careers as company managers may still be members of the company managers' union, the Association of Theatrical Press Agents and Managers (ATPAM), which is also known as the International Alliance of Theatrical Stage Employees (IATSE) Local 18032.

Artistic Director

Artistic directors work primarily in the not-for-profit theater. Under the direction of the board of directors, the artistic director creates and implements the artistic focus of a theater company. To that end, the artistic director (AD) hires and supervises directors, performers, designers, stage managers, and others. The AD typically chooses the season program, develops a budget with the managing director/executive director, and is usually the public spokesperson for the organization and involved in fund-raising. This person may direct some or all of the group's theater productions. In some smaller, developing companies that do not have managing director positions yet, the artistic director will also perform some or all of the duties of the managing director.

Typically artistic directors begin as theater directors. The founding force for many not-for-profit theaters is their first artistic director. Some business or arts management training is highly desirable. Compensation varies with the not-for-profit theater's budget size. With beginning companies, the artistic director may not receive any salary. Among the largest not-for-profit theater organizations, salaries can be substantial. For example, André Bishop, artistic director of Lincoln Center Theatre, is paid more than $400,000 yearly. In 2007 Joe Dowling, artistic director of the Guthrie Theater in Minneapolis, was paid more than $680,000. Each of these NFP theaters has a yearly budget usually in excess of $30 million.

There is no union, as the artistic director is considered upper management. If the artistic director began as a director, membership may be maintained in the Stage Directors and Choreographers Society.

Executive Director

The executive director may be called managing director, chief administrative officer, or business manager. This position exists primarily in the not-for-profit theater.

The executive director works side-by-side with the artistic director overseeing the administrative side of the organization. Under the direction of the board of directors, the executive director coordinates the day-to-day and overall company operations, typically including fund-raising, ticket sales, community relations, education programming, office management, human resources, and volunteer management. In many cases the executive director—together with the artistic director—represents the theater to the larger public. The executive director identifies and cultivates major donors and sponsors and directs the maintenance of the donor database; identifies grants, and prepares grant applications. The executive director creates, manages, and reports operating budgets and ensures that there are adequate financial and management controls.

Additional duties might include compiling production information for graphic designers; supervising loans of costumes, props, and construction materials; and training volunteers. If the theater has an education area, the managing director coordinates with the education staff regarding marketing, budgeting, and collection of income from education activities.

Many theaters will require a managing director to have a B.A. or B.S. degree, preferably with a concentration in business management, accounting, or other similar discipline, or, better, a master of business administration (M.B.A.)—sometimes the M.B.A. is in arts administration—or a master of fine arts (M.F.A.) in arts administration. Previous experience with not-for-profit organization business operations, with not-for-profit grant applications, and with public speaking are also preferred. In some cases a familiarity with the theater's community is deemed important by the board of directors.

Salary varies with the size of the organization. When searching for a managing director in 2010, the Profile Theatre published a salary range of $32,000 to $35,000 per year. The Profile Theatre's 2008 IRS filing shows a total budget of more than $388,000. Lincoln Center Theatre's executive director, Bernard Gersten, working for a not-for-profit theater with a budget in excess of $35 million, received more than $400,000 in 2008.

Literary Manager or Dramaturg

Literary managers work primarily in the not-for-profit theater. A literary manager/dramaturg (LM/D) has varied duties, depending on what parts of the job the artistic director or production director cares to do personally and depending on the size and sophistication of the not-for-profit theater. The LM/D may help develop the mission of the theater company and help plan the season. The LM/D looks for scripts, new and classic, and may solicit scripts from writers, and sometimes prepares adaptations and translations. For a given production, the LM/D may locate versions of the script, cut or edit scripts, secure permissions to use other copyrighted material, and find music, pictures, and videos. Historical research for the director, actors, and designers can be part of the job as can be identifying ideas for marketing. The LM/D may create lobby exhibits and write introductory material for the program as well as collaborate with the education director on school-focused materials. A dramaturg typically has an advanced degree, usually at least an M.A., that focuses on theater literature, theater criticism, or theater history.

There is no union of dramaturgs. The professional association is the Literary Managers & Dramaturgs of the Americas (LMDA). Literary managers or dramaturgs who are also playwrights may belong to the Dramatists Guild of America, a trade group but not a union. The LMDA reported that a 1999 survey showed that most literary managers/dramaturgs received salaries ranging from $28,600 to $39,000. The report proposes as a general guideline for freelance engagements that LM/Ds should receive at least one-half of a director's salary.

Positions typically reporting to the literary manager/dramaturg include script reader, reading series manager, education director, teaching artist, and archivist.

Company Manager

At its core the company manager job is administrative. Company managers are responsible for the *offstage* needs of all production staff. They may be responsible for getting contracts signed by actors and others and for distributing paychecks. For touring productions or out-of-town tryouts, they arrange travel and housing. They may be called on in emergencies, driving cast members to a hospital in case of illness or securing a flight home in case of a death in the family. In the not-for-profit theater, the company manager's duties may flow into the duties of a general manager. Rachel Blavatnik, associate producer/company manager for Florida's NFP Maltz Jupiter Theatre said, "On any given day, my job description runs the gambit of administrator, counselor, chauffeur, cook, and even maid."

Beverly Edwards was company manager for a commercial revival on Broadway of *Hamlet* that starred movie actor Jude Law. She stated that during the production the paparazzi "didn't find his apartment for a couple of months but once they did they staked it out. One night, I'm not exaggerating; there were 200 paparazzi outside the building. I said, well, he can't be late, he's Hamlet! So I had to hire 4 policemen to go down there and surround him so he could get to his car." Ms. Edwards's anecdote shows that company manager is a job both routine and improvisatory.

The company manager's union is the Association of Theatrical Press Agents and Managers (ATPAM), or IATSE Local 18032. Company managers usually began elsewhere in theater and then discovered a gift for administration. ATPAM doesn't publish its minimum salaries to nonmembers. A copy of the 2002 agreement we located for off-Broadway productions shows a minimum salary in a 400 to 499–seat house of $1,018 per week plus union fees. Broadway fees are certainly higher.

Technical Director, Technical Supervisor, or Technical Manager

Typically the title of technical director (TD) is used for two related but different jobs: one for a theater building and another for a specific production. In either case the TD is foremost a manager of technical staff but may in small venues have responsibility for direct labor in building, painting, and crewing a show. When hired for a theater building, the TD keeps theater equipment functional and safe; maintains floor plans, sound and lighting plans, and equipment inventories for the theater building; and communicates and coordinates with the technical staff for each production. In the case that a theater licenses its auditorium to traveling shows, the TD assists in load-in and load-out of the traveling show's scenery and lights. When a touring production books a venue, the venue's technical director will review measurements, floor plans, electrical availability, fly systems, and the like to ensure that the set can be accommodated. In every venue a touring show lands, there will be the need for communication, coordination, and problem-solving between the venue's TD and the tour's technical staff. In some cases a not-for-profit theater's overall technical director will also be the technical director for individual productions as well.

The technical director for a specific production coordinates with the director and design staff to help determine how scenery is to be constructed and also monitors scenery budgets. The TD in a not-for-profit theater may make technical drawings based on the scenery designer's drawings, nowadays almost always using computer drafting software and, in doing so, solves technical, engineering, safety, and budget problems as they arise. The TD may direct the carpentry shop staff, electricians, fly crews, stage crews, and so on. Depending on the production, a TD may also supervise lighting and sound installation and operation and any pyrotechnics. During a run a TD may check that everything is operating correctly and safely and instigate renovations where necessary.

Technical directors in the past have usually risen to the position via on-the-job training in qualifying positions. Increasingly an M.F.A. in technical theater along with experience in subordinate positions is required. Subordinate positions might include head carpenter, head rigger, and the like. Capability with computer-aided design is very important. Technical directors may be members of the United States Institute for Theatre Technology (USITT), a trade organization. There is no union.

Director of Production or Head of Production

This job title is found mostly in the not-for-profit theatre. The director of production typically supervises production office staff, stage management, company management, production shops, and facilities. This person may negotiate with unions and develop and monitor the production budget.

Director of Finance or Chief Financial Officer or, Rarely, Controller

This job title is found primarily in the not-for-profit theater. The director of finance (DF) directs, manages, and hires staff related to financial operations, often including budgeting, accounts payable and receivable, accounting and bookkeeping, banking, ticketing operations, computer operations, fund-raising, and more. The DF develops and monitors controls to assure that financial functions have integrity. Reports are compiled for the board of directors on financial issues. One of the most important responsibilities is cash management, since an organization's need for cash on a day-to-day basis can be different from the daily availability of cash, even for a not-for-profit organization operating with a yearly surplus.

Many theaters will require a director of finance to have a B.A. or B.S. degree preferably with a concentration in business management, accounting, or a similar discipline, or, better, a master of business administration (M.B.A.), perhaps in arts administration, or an M.F.A. in Arts Administration. Previous experience with not-for-profit organizations business operations is preferred.

Development Director

The development director works solely in the not-for-profit theater. The development director manages fund-raising. Managing the theater's fundraising may include responsibility for the membership process, corporate sponsorships, applying for grants, maintaining donor computer records, and coordination of special events. The development director is the primary source of the theater's fundraising plan and budget, identifies and develops potential donors, and coordinates with the board of directors in its efforts related to direct giving and fund-raising. Public speaking is typically part of the job as is writing individual or mass-mail letters, brochures, public service advertisements, parts of the annual report, website text, and the like. In a large organization, the development director may direct a large staff; in smaller ones the development director may have no direct reporting staff or may even be expected to accomplish larger objectives while working on a part-time basis. Subordinate positions may include a director of individual giving, a director of special events, and others.

Theaters will seek candidates with significant knowledge and experience in fund-raising and, in larger organizations where the development director has subordinate staff, some management experience. Specific experience in not-for-profit theater and/or the local not-for-profit fund-raising environment is often preferred.

Director of Marketing and Sales Promotion

The director of marketing supervises all marketing, which might include season and individual production marketing initiatives; media communications, including website development; long-term efforts in audience development, including capturing audience research; and marketing budget management.

Marketing Manager

The marketing manager plans and directs the marketing activities of the theater or production by brand marketing, event marketing, audience development campaigns, and audience surveys and consults on season planning, develops or consults on all publications such as brochures, newsletters, direct mail, digital media, press releases, advertisements, and posters. This person monitors sales and reports on marketing results.

Other Management Positions

This listing cannot include all the management positions that might be hired by a large theater producing organization, whether commercial or not-for-profit. Any of these positions may have assistants, associates, and deputies. There will be office support jobs, such as office manager, secretary, administrative assistant, and receptionist. Some other management positions include

Director of sales operations
Digital marketing manager
Publications manager
Graphic designer
Ticket services manager
Box office manager
Group sales manager
Box office associate
Grant writer
Director of individual giving
Special events director
Script reader
Reading series manager
Archivist

Artistic Jobs
Director

The director is primarily responsible for all artistic issues in a production. Directors work with and through the other theater artists—designers, actors, and technical staff—to develop a creative and unified interpretation of the script and a satisfying experience for audiences. The director plans the physical production with designers, rehearses the company of actors, and supervises technical rehearsals, all within established budget limits. In the commercial theater, directors perform some of the functions that the *dramaturg* or *literary manager* would perform in the not-for-profit theater, that is, script development with the playwright, script analysis and interpretation, historical research, and the like.

During a long run the director is required to visit the show on a regular basis and may call brush-up rehearsals and cast and direct replacements. The director also stages touring productions. In some cases these tasks, which may take place after a show opens, are primarily done by assistant directors with the director coming in near the end of the process for final input.

In practice some producers in the commercial theater and artistic directors in the not-for-profit theater will want a more-or-less collaborative role in some artistic issues. For example, producers and artistic directors often have approval of casting decisions, especially dismissal of actors before opening. Producers and artistic directors almost always are involved in artistic decisions affecting budgets and marketing.

Stage directing is increasingly seen as a discipline separate from other theater disciplines, and, for rising directors, an M.F.A. is the most appropriate degree. However, some directors still migrate to the field from acting or stage management.

The Stage Directors and Choreographers Society (SDC) represents directors and choreographers. The union has 1,900 members and 500 associate members. Associate membership is available to early career directors and/or choreographers, college and university professionals, and community theater artists.

Union minimum fees vary with the nature of the engagement and are highly detailed. Of course, an artist may be able to negotiate a higher fee. In addition to these payments, producers are required to make contributions to the union's pension fund and to the member's health insurance. SDC Broadway minimum in the 2007–8 season for director of a musical was a $35,740 advance against royalties plus a fee of $23,830 spread over the rehearsal period. Basic royalties were 0.75 percent of gross receipts or 3.5 percent of net weekly operating profit until recoupment and 3.85 percent after recoupment with a minimum of $920 weekly. For a nonmusical play, the advance against royalties was $22,490 plus a fee of $28,795.

About the League of Resident Theatres (LORT)

LORT was founded to promote the general welfare of professional resident theaters in the United States, to encourage relations among resident theaters, to provide resident theaters with opportunities to act in their common interests, and to represent its members in labor relations.

LORT has seventy-six active members in twenty-nine states and the District of Columbia. According to the LORT website, "LORT Theatres collectively issue more Equity contracts to actors than Broadway and commercial tours combined." All LORT theaters are not-for-profit corporations with at least twelve playing weeks.

The theaters are classed for contract purposes by budget size, with LORT-A theaters generally being the largest. LORT-A include the Milwaukee Repertory Theater; Ford's Theatre in Washington, D.C.; American Conservatory Theater in San Francisco; and Center Theatre Group in Los Angeles. The LORT-A+ theatres are the three so-called super NFPs that, as previously mentioned, produce in Broadway houses and so are eligible for Tony Awards: Lincoln Center Theater, the Manhattan Theatre Club, and the Roundabout Theatre.

LORT-C theaters, the second smallest of the classifications, have budgets between $45,000 and $69,999. Budget ranges for LORT-D, the smallest of the League's theaters, are not published.

About the word *resident:* in the past many regional theaters hired companies of artists who were resident in the community throughout the season. This still happens now at some summer theaters, such as the many Shakespeare theaters in rural areas about the country, but most regional theaters hire artists for one show at a time. Still, the term *resident* has stuck for LORT.

Consider the rates for the smallest of the League of Resident Theaters (LORT) theaters, the LORT-D. The union minimum for a director in a LORT-D theater was $6,344 per production as of 2009, and if rehearsals extend beyond four weeks and three days, an additional $171 per day.

Choreographer

Choreographers create dances and musical movement and train the cast in executing the dances and moves. They also coordinate costuming and lighting with the dance movements, working with the respective designers. During a long run the choreographer may call brush-up rehearsals and cast and teach replacements. Touring productions are usually staged by the same person who staged the original show. In some cases these tasks, which take place after a show opens, are primarily done by assistant choreographers with the choreographer coming in near the end of the process for final input.

Choreographers generally begin their careers as dancers. Dancing is grueling, and choreography can be a way for dancers to extend their careers past the point where professional dancing is physically challenging. Dance training typically begins in youth and professional engagements may come as early as seventeen or eighteen years of age. Some colleges and universities award bachelor's or master's degrees in dance, but a degree is not generally considered a requirement to be a dancer or choreographer. We could find no university degree program specifically in choreography.

Choreographers are represented by the Stage Directors and Choreographers Society (SDC). Union minimums vary with the nature of the engagement and are highly detailed. Of course, an artist may be able to negotiate a higher return. In addition to these payments, producers are required to make contributions to the union's pension fund and to the member's health insurance. SDC minimum payments for a Broadway choreographer in 2007–8 were a $29,785 advance against royalties plus a $19,730 fee. Royalties for a choreographer were 0.5 percent of gross receipts or 1 percent of weekly operating profit until recoupment and 1.1 percent after recoupment, with a minimum weekly payment of $475. In LORT-D engagements the minimum for a choreographer was 75 percent of the director's minimum.

Designer

The professional theater has many kinds of designers, including set designer; costume designer; lighting designer; sound designer; projections or media designer; hair, wig, and makeup designer; and puppet and mask designer.

Designers work with the director to develop a concept for the production and read the script to determine location, set, and/or historical requirements. Costume, set, and projection designers research historical sources. They prepare a series of drawings with increasing levels of detail. A set designer will usually build scale models of the design, costume designers select fabric, and set designers also select furniture, rugs, and the like. All designers estimate costs and make changes where necessary to meet the budget. Designers work with contractors or their own staff to have scenery and costumes built or sound and lighting equipment rented. Designers are involved at installation and technical rehearsals to solve problems. Sound designers deal with amplification, especially for musicals, and may find or compose and record incidental music for nonmusical plays along with sound effects. In long runs or tours, designers may be involved in creating replacements for worn designs; this is especially true for costuming in musicals. Set designers today need experience in computer-aided design (CAD).

The designers' union, United Scenic Artists, also known as International Alliance of Theatrical Stage Employees (IATSE) Local 829, defines typical job duties for some designers as part of its contract with the Broadway League. Scenic designer duties IATSE include

(1) To complete either a working model of the settings to scale or to complete color sketches or color sketch models of the settings and necessary working drawings for the constructing carpenter at the reasonable discretion of the producer.

(2) To supply the contracting painter with color schemes or color sketches sufficient for the contracting painter.

(3) To design or select or approve properties required for the production, including draperies and furniture.

(4) To design and/or supervise special scenic effects for the production, including projections.

(5) To supply specifications for the constructing carpenter, to supervise the building and painting of sets and the making of properties and, at the request of the producer, discuss estimates for the same with contractors satisfactory to the producer, such estimates to be submitted to the producer at a specific time. If the designer is required to participate in more than three estimating sessions of each class, extra compensation shall be

paid as mutually agreed upon by the designer and producer subject to the union's approval, which shall not be unreasonably withheld.

(6) To be present at pre-Broadway and Broadway setups, technical and dress rehearsals, the first public performances and openings out-of-town, the first public performance and opening in New York and to conduct the scenic rehearsals therefore, as may be reasonably requested by the producer, in accordance with industry past practice.

(7) To attend public performances from time to time for the purpose of conducting a 'normal check' of the sets. This provision shall not be applied in an unreasonable manner.

Costume designer duties include

(1) To submit a costume plot of the production listing costume changes by scene for each character in the cast.

(2) To provide color sketches of all costumes designed for the production and any form of a visual representation for costumes selected for the production.

(3) To supply for the contracting costume shop complete color sketches or outline sketches with color samples attached, including drawings or necessary descriptions of detail and its application, sufficient for the contracting costume shop.

(4) To participate in not more than three estimating sessions with costume shops of the producer's choice for the execution of the designs if so requested. If the designer is required to obtain more than three estimates for the same costumes, extra compensation shall be paid as mutually agreed upon by the designer and producer subject to the union's approval, which shall not be unreasonable withheld.

(5) To be responsible for the selection and coordination of all contemporary costumes worn in the production including selection from performers' personal wardrobe where such situation arises.

(6) To be responsible for the supervision of all necessary fittings and alterations of the costumes.

(7) To design, select and/or approve all costume accessories such as headgear, gloves, footwear, hose, purses, jewelry, umbrellas, canes, fans, bouquets, and the like.

(8) To supervise and/or approve hair styling and selection of wigs, hairpieces, mustaches, and beards.

(9) To be present at pre-Broadway and Broadway technical and dress rehearsals, the first public performance and openings out of town, the first public performance and opening in New York and to conduct costume rehearsals therefore, as may be reasonably requested by the producer in accordance with industry past practice.

(10) To attend public performances from time to time for the purpose of conducting a 'normal check' of the costumes. This provision shall not be applied in an unreasonable manner.

Lighting designer duties include

(1) To provide a full equipment list and light plot drawn to scale showing type and position of all instruments necessary to accomplish lighting design.
(2) To provide color plot and all necessary information required by the contract electrician.
(3) To provide control plot showing allocation of instruments for lighting control.
(4) To supervise and plot special effects.
(5) To supply specifications and to obtain estimates for the same for the Producer from contractors satisfactory to the producers, such estimates to be submitted tothe Producer at a specific time. If the designer is required to obtain more than three estimates, extra compensation shall be paid as mutually agreed upon between designer and producer subject to the union's approval, which shall not be unreasonably withheld.
(6) To supervise hanging and focusing of the lighting equipment, and the setting up of all lighting cues.
(7) To be present at pre-Broadway and Broadway setups, technical and dress rehearsals, the first public performances and openings out of town, the first public performance and opening in New York and to conduct the lighting rehearsals therefor as may be reasonably requested by the producer, in accordance with industry past practice. In the event the out of town stops prior to the Broadway opening are more than three, and the lighting designer's presence is required by the producer, the lighting designer shall be paid the daily rate up to a maximum of four days for each stop beyond three. It is understood and agreed that this shall not apply to scenic and costume designers.
(8) To attend public performances from time to time for the purpose of conducting a "normal check" of the lighting. This provision shall not be applied in an unreasonable manner.

In the United States theater designers are typically trained in university theater departments. In Europe training is more likely to be in a fine art or studio art school. It is rare that bachelor of arts or bachelor of fine arts degrees (B.A. or B.F.A.) are offered specifically in design. The degree of choice is the master of fine arts (M.F.A.). However, that degree is not required. One popular theater designer, David Rockwell (*Hairspray, All Shook Up, Legally Blonde*), trained as an architect and still works primarily in architecture and interior design.

Union minimums for designers vary with the nature of the engagement. Of course an artist may be able to negotiate a higher payment. In addition to these minimums in table 2, producers are required to make contributions to the union's pension fund and to the member's health insurance.

Table 2: Broadway Union Minimums for
a Musical with Multiple Sets, 2008

	Advance against royalties	Fee	Royalty
Set designer	$6,291	$29,525	$380 per week or
Costume designer	$6,291	$19,525	0.461 percent of
Lighting designer	$4,720	$22,144	weekly net profit

Note: Broadway designers receive a royalty for each week a production runs, based on the minimums of union contracts.

Union minimums for sound designers and projection designers on Broadway have not been published by Local 829.

For contrast, the fees for not-for-profit LORT-C engagements were for set designer $3,011, costume designer $3,011, lighting designer $2,458, and sound designer $2,548. There are no published rates for LORT-D engagements.

Production Stage Manager/Stage Manager

The stage manager works with the director to establish the organization and duties for the stage crew during technical rehearsals, and the stage manager "runs" the show by giving cues to light and sound board operators, stagehands, actors, and others. In some instances where a show has employed both a production stage manager and a stage manager, the production stage manager is the head stage manager. However, this terminology is not universal. Some shows use the terms *stage manager* and *assistant stage manager*.

Actors' Equity Association (Equity), the union for actors and stage managers, defines the duties of stage managers as:

> coordinating a production during rehearsal and performance periods; maintaining the artistic intentions of the director after the opening of the show; scheduling understudy or brush-up rehearsals; and, with the deputy, maintaining order within the company. The stage manager also assembles and maintains the prompt book (the accurate playing/stage business text), cue sheets, plots, and other necessary daily records. Additionally, the stage manager maintains records of attendance, illness, injury, changes in duties, and other work-related issues.

Coordinating a production during rehearsal and performance periods often involves more than scheduling and communicating with all staff. In many production situations, the stage manager will act as the director's assistant during rehearsals, recording the director's decisions about blocking and recording other notes for staff of all kinds, thus enabling the director to concentrate on directing.

During performance the stage manager calls the cues for actors and crew over headphones and dressing-room speakers. The stage manager may contact understudies and standbys and may rehearse replacement actors, especially for small roles. In some venues the stage manager may call and direct brush-up rehearsals during a long run. When scenery or costumes need refurbishment, the stage manager is usually the one responsible to initiate action from others working for the production. The stage manager is the first point of contact for issues of safety. On a tour the stage manager or production stage manager often supervises the movement of scenery, costumes, sound equipment, and lighting into and out of a theater, that is, "load-in" and "load-out."

While some courses in stage management are offered at the B.A. degree level, intensive training in stage management is usually offered at the B.F.A. or M.F.A. level. Stage managers also advance from subordinate or intern positions, especially in the not-for-profit theater.

In Equity situations the stage manager serves as shop foreman. As such, the stage manager is the local expert on Equity work rules. This requires of the stage manager a dual allegiance: assistant to the director and union leader for the actors. Perhaps as a result of the dual allegiance, the company also elects a deputy from among the acting company whose duties, according to Equity, are as follows:

> The deputy advises performers on procedures and rules, and directs problems to the stage manager and/or the Equity staff. Deputies and members should not take grievances or questions about working conditions or rules directly to management. Once alerted to a problem, the stage manager or the Equity business representative will contact management. . . . The deputy and the stage manager advise Equity of possible rule infractions, complaints, or any questions that company members may have.

In addition to Equity, there is a professional group, the Stage Manager's Association. Stage managers may also be members of a professional association, the United States Institute for Theatre Technology (USITT).

The Equity minimum pay for a stage manager on Broadway is $2,637 a week as of the 2009–2010 season. For LORT theaters, the fees vary by the theater's budget size. As of February 2010 the minimums ranged from the largest, LORT-A, with an Equity minimum of $1,254, to the smallest, LORT-D, with an Equity minimum of $683 weekly. (For a description of LORT theaters, see the sidebar on page 21.)

Casting Director

The casting director evaluates roles in a script and make lists of potential actors for major roles or roles with unusual requirements, such as children, little people, and others. Sometimes the casting director conducts initial auditions, culling the possibilities to present only a limited number of choices for the producer and director to see in callbacks. Casting directors typically see a lot of theater and are familiar with the talent that is available. Their professional association is the Casting Society of America (CSA), which represents casting professionals in theater, television, and film.

Actor

An actor portrays a role or roles in a play or musical, interpreting character traits and fulfilling the part's dramatic function. An actor rehearses, working with the director and other actors to develop an effective performance. Of course, the actor memorizes lines and stage business including special skills such as sword fighting, and he or she may be called on to move scenery when essential to the director/designer concept. In a musical the actor may sing and/or dance. In audition notices the casting director may call for "dancers who sing" or "singers who dance," indicating in each case by the first listed duty where the actors' main talent should lie. The Equity contract with the Broadway League defines the duties of an actor as:

> The actor agrees to be prompt at rehearsals and to appear at the theatre no later than one half-hour prior to the performance; to pay strict regard to make-up and dress; to perform actor's services as reasonably directed to the best of actor's ability; to properly care for actor's costume and props; when required by the producer to wear and use electronic equipment; to respect the physical property of the production and the theatre; and to abide by all reasonable rules and regulations of the producer not in conflict with Equity Rules.

Equity also defines some special actor roles, such as

Understudy. Understudy assignments are required to cover for principal performers' roles in case of sickness or other emergency.

Chorus. A separate contract is used for actors whose primary function is chorus.

Swing. A swing is a nonperforming member of the chorus who substitutes for absent chorus members. A partial swing is a performing member of the chorus who is assigned to "swing" specific production numbers for absent chorus members.

Extra. An extra provides atmosphere and background and may not be identified as a specific character. The extra receives a reduced salary, usually
50 percent of the minimum.

Fight Captain. A fight captain is a company member responsible for maintaining the fight choreography and safety.

Dance Captain. The dance captain is the member of the company who maintains the artistic standards of all musical staging and choreography. The
dance captain rehearses understudies, swings, and replacement performers.

In Broadway shows that have no book, that is, no written script, but are made of
all dancing, sometimes dancers are represented by the American Guild of Musical Artists, which represents singers of opera and dancers of ballet. Generally,
however, in theater dancers are members of Equity.

Fight Choreographer or Fight Director

The fight choreographer designs, teaches, and directs physical conflict, including slaps, hand-to-hand fighting, sword fighting, and using firearms so that it all
is convincing but safe for the actors. Fight choreographers usually have a background in acting and developed an interest in and training for fight choreography
over time. The Society of American Fight Directors is a professional association,
offering training and standards for fight choreographers.

Dialect Coach

A dialect coach works with actors on vocal production, pronunciation, or speaking rhythm, sometimes to correct flaws in the actor's speech and other times to
teach the actor an accent or dialect. In some shows the dialect coach may serve as
an acting coach, working with individual actors, under the guidance of the director, to make acting choices. This person may help actors to memorize lines. The
best dialect coaches can find work easily. Elizabeth "Liz" Smith is highly regarded
in this area and has been credited as dialect coach, vocal consultant, or vocal
coach on more than twenty Broadway productions just since the start of this
millennium. Her career as a dialect coach on Broadway dates back to 1974, and
she also works for regional NFP theaters.

Dresser

Dressers help in maintaining wardrobes and wigs and assist in quick changes.
Depending on the size of the show, there may be as many as fifteen dressers, with
typical weekly salaries of $1,100 to $1,400. A star performer may have a long and
personal connection to his or her dresser, requiring that dresser to be hired for a
show if the dresser is available. When Sutton Foster won the Tony Award for best
actress in a musical in spring 2011, her thank you speech included her dresser.

"He's moving to Cape Cod, and . . . I love you so much!" she gushed about her dresser, Julien Havard. Later Foster explained, "We're like best friends, brother and sister. He sees the best, the worst, the good, the bad. There's no one in the world I'm more comfortable with than him." The actress Patti LuPone said, "If you've got a great dresser, then you've got a really wonderful backstage atmosphere. If you have a real lousy dresser, then people are bitching."

Technical/Crew Jobs

Technical or crew positions include a range of jobs. Some of those listed here require experience or training and some are entry-level positions.

Head carpenter or master carpenter
Automation carpenter
Head electrician or master electrician
Followspot operator
Light board operator
Electrician
Deck electrician
Head sound
Production prop supervisor or prop master
Prop-monkey
Costumer
Wardrobe supervisor or wardrobe manager or wardrobe mistress/master
Draper
Tailor
Milliner
Wardrobe crafts
Hair/makeup
Stitchers
Hair supervisor
Scenery supervisor

Theater Support Jobs

As noted, in the commercial theater, the theater building is not the responsibility of the producer or those the producer hires. In the not-for-profit theater, however, theater buildings are leased or owned and so require staff for their management, maintenance, and upkeep. These positions may include

Operations managers
Office manager
Receptionist

Information technology director
Database administrator/programmer
House carpenter
House electrician
Theater building manager
House manager
Head usher/ushers
Security
Maintenance/janitorial services
Lobby refreshment/souvenirs sale

Education Jobs

In the not-for-profit theater, often the organization sees it as advantageous to perform outreach and education to school-age children. Some develop and distribute teacher manuals, lesson plans, and the like to local schools so that the theater's productions can be used in the school curriculum. (Commercial theaters sometimes prepare, print, and distribute teacher guides; they typically hire temporary consultants to prepare these teaching materials.) In addition, some not-for-profit theaters form alliances with university theater programs that provide student interns to work in the not-for-profit programs. These interns require some educational support. This leads to a class of jobs distinct from others in a theater. They may include an education director and a teaching artist, among other positions.

One NFP theater that boasts of the quality and extent its education program is Roundabout Theatre in New York City. During the 2009–10 season, Roundabout's education program had a budget of $1.2 million. It employed forty-five teaching artists for a total of nearly 7,000 working hours. Roundabout has a program of school partnerships with New York City public schools that have few resources for theater education. This program provides workshops from its teaching artists and free tickets for students to attend Roundabout performances. In total it distributed more than 6,600 free or discounted tickets to public school students. Students at risk of dropping out of school were recruited for the Roundabout after-school program in which the students wrote and produced two plays. Every student involved graduated from high school. Roundabout conducts theater workshops for public teachers. Roundabout has a paid career development program—internship—offering hands-on experience for young professionals in theater administration or production. Few NFP theaters have as varied and well-funded an education program as the Roundabout has, but its example provides a sense of the range of education activities that NFP theaters might perform. These activities require specialized staffing.

Consultants/Services

For some services commercial and not-for-profit theaters turn to consulting firms instead of maintaining staff within their organizations. Few producers or not-for-profit theaters need a full time attorney on staff, so they retain lawyers as consultants. There are, for example, legal firms that specialize in copyright law, entertainment law, or theater law. Chambers and Partners, a law firm rating organization, lists seven theater law firms in the New York area. Similarly a theater producer or not-for-profit group may not have a full-time advertising staff. In New York City advertising for commercial theater is dominated by three firms, Spotco, Serino Coyne, and the smallest one, Eliran Murphy Group. There's also an Internet design firm that specializes in theater, Situation Interactive.

Some typical consultants, services firms, and supplies used by theater include the following:

Press agent or press representative
Marketing
Advertising
Photographer
Signage and displays
Website design, maintenance, "interactive marketing"
Information technology
Casting
Payroll
Accounting
Insurance, risk management
Banking
Legal counsel
Immigration counsel
Government relations
House physician, physical therapist
Merchandising
Copyright clearances
Travel services
Security
Lobby refreshments, merchandising
Scenery construction
Scenery automation
Lighting equipment supply
Sound equipment supply
Costume construction

Custom footwear
Custom head wear

Playwrights

Playwrights, arguably the most important contributor to success in theater, are not employees, according to court rulings. The Internal Revenue Service is concerned with the definition of employee because employees, as distinct from independent contractors, require collection of interim income taxes, payment of Social Security and Medicare taxes, unemployment taxes, and more. The definition is not totally precise but is based on a number of questions, such as

> Does the worker determine where and when work will be done?
> Does the worker provide the tools needed for the job?
> Is the relationship between payer and worker temporary or occasional or
> essentially permanent?

The answers to all these questions for the playwright—"yes," "yes," and "occasional"—determines that the playwright is not an employee of the theater producer. The playwright writes whenever, wherever, using whatever tools are at hand. A producer generally agrees to produce only a single work of the playwright's. This determination that the playwright is not an employee is historically strengthened because the group representing playwrights, the Dramatists Guild of America, in its early years chose not to be identified as a labor organization. As a result the Dramatists Guild cannot enforce its model contracts with either its own members or with producers. To do so would expose it to legal action for restraint of trade. This distinction between contractor and employee also holds for composers and lyricists. Both composers and lyricists are members of the Dramatists Guild.

When a producer is interested in a playwright's work, the producer obtains an option from the playwright. The option gives the producer the exclusive right to produce the work for a certain period of time, usually six months, in exchange for a cash payment to the playwright. The producer can extend the option with additional payments. If the producer stages the work under certain conditions, the producer garners other subsidiary rights in the work, including the right to stage tours and international productions, a share of the playwright's income from other productions, movie sales, merchandising, and other sources for many years thereafter.

Each player in the option between producer and playwright gives something that the other cannot. The producer offers special skills in organizing investors and other creative artists to get a play on stage. In doing so, the producer takes on the risk that the production might fail, the investment might be lost, and the subsidiary rights acquired from the playwright might have no value. The playwright offers a unique creative work but usually does not have the resources or the expertise to see that work produced successfully on the stage. The producer's investment increases the value of the playwright's work and that is the argument for sharing future income.

Beyond the Facts

There are hundreds of theater careers available to those who are educated, trained, and eager to begin at the beginning. Clearly there are more theater jobs off-stage than on-stage. Off-stage workers are essential to make a production come alive for each performance, to make sure there is an audience to see the performance and, in the not-for-profit theater, to sustain and grow the organization. And there are even more types of jobs being created in theater over time.

In almost all cases, the established NFP theaters with significant budgets hire more people than the commercial theater because they are ongoing, continuing enterprises. The commercial theater, however, may use different titles than the NFP theater to describe the same general job duties. In both the commercial and NFP theaters, some workers have an employee-employer relationship with the producer or NFP theater and thus can be represented by unions. Others cannot.

We were surprised to realize how many traditional professionals, ones not usually associated with theater production, work to make theater. Commercial and NFP theaters need accountants, bookkeepers, secretaries, and the like. There are lawyers and law firms specializing in theatrical law, orthopedic doctors specializing in treating dancers' injuries, and public relations and marketing firms representing individual productions or NFP companies. The list goes on.

Beyond the facts lie opinions. Here are a few of ours. In some NFP theater jobs, there is an implied career ladder. For example, a head carpenter may be promoted to technical director when a job opens. Sometimes NFP producers or production managers rise to become general managers or executive managers. In the commercial theater, this kind of promotion/advancement is less common if for no other reason than that the commercial theater is not organized as a continuing corporation.

Artistic jobs—actors, directors, designers—prosper from successful collaboration in any theater. Success breeds more potential access to future jobs. Of course, people with the power to influence hiring often choose to work with the same people when possible because they know their strengths, communication styles, and personalities. Playwrights may choose to work with the directors they know, directors may choose designers and actors who are known to them, technical directors may engage the carpenters, painters, and stagehands who have delivered for the theater before, and so on. The talented and easy-to-work-with become known and are more likely to be hired. The difficult and sluggish are less likely to be hired again. This is not unique to the theater world: no one chooses to work with loudmouths and loafers. However, the theater world in the United States is relatively small, and word gets around. The inference from this should be that every job a theater person gets should be engaged with the knowledge that one's performance can lead to a subsequent job—or make landing a subsequent job harder.

CHAPTER 2

Theater Education Offers Many Paths

There are many paths one can take after high school graduation to pursue a theater career. The surprising fact is that many high school drama teachers and guidance counselors are unable to communicate a clear understanding of the alternatives, their interconnections, and their impact on the likelihood of success in the field and thus steer students to an appropriate path. A survey undertaken by the nonprofit group Public Agenda found that "most students, even those who successfully complete university, give their high school guidance counselors fair or poor ratings" on the quality of university advice the counselors offered. This section of *Theater Careers* presents an overview of the choices in education open to those interested in a career in theater. The choices include going directly into the professional theater or earning an undergraduate university degree, and then a graduate degree. A flowchart of the choices is set forth in fig. 3.

Directly from High School to Work

High school graduates can attempt to find work in theater directly from high school without additional training (See item ① in fig. 3.) Some backstage jobs have no extra educational requirements, although they may have work experience or union membership requirements in some markets. These jobs include stagehand, rigger, dresser, hairdresser, costume supervisor, and carpenter. People with experience in sewing and tailoring or in hairdressing might find work in the shops of designers. Draftsmen or artists and computer draftsmen or computer artists might find work in the studios of theater designers. For the actual designers of sets, scenery, sound, and costumes, additional training and experience are generally essential. There is both an art and a technology of design that is not usually taught in high school.

The least risky way to begin to garner that experience and expertise is in a school environment. For designers and directors, higher education plus some experience gathered as an intern or assistant is virtually always necessary before a producer or artistic director will entrust a production to a first-time talent. Although experienced *actors* often attempt to direct plays—and some are successful—directing requires experience and expertise in managing companies of

Education Paths to Work or Teach in the Theater

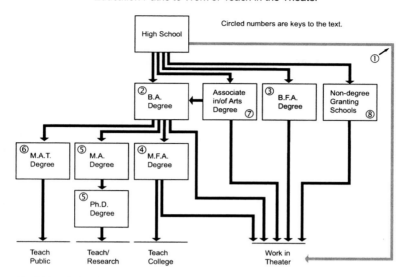

Fig. 3. The choices for advanced schooling are many. Some degrees are prerequisites for other degrees. A high school graduate interested in a career in theater has four education possibilities. A holder of a bachelor of arts degree interested in further training has three choices. This chart is discussed in detail throughout this chapter and those discussions are keyed to the circled numbers on this chart.

artists, planning rehearsals and production meetings, communicating with other creative staff, and interpreting scripts and stories, which most actors do not nec-essarily develop.

Many high school graduates, particularly those who want to be actors, buoyed by success on their high school or community theater stages, go directly from home to a major city to seek work. There are a number of successful performers whose careers began without post-secondary-school training, but in general this is a path riddled with disappointment. Going from being a star on a small-town stage—a big fish in a little pond—to competing in auditions against trained and experienced performers is bound to be a profound challenge.

Professionals in the know—casting directors and agents—strongly encourage additional training. Many say that, in reviewing resumes, they make a first cut by eliminating those that don't show training after secondary school. They reason that whereas post-high-school education is no guarantee of capability, it at least shows ambition and devotion to a career. New York–based casting director Dave Clemmons said, "It's not so much where you trained; it's just that you did it. There are so few people out there who can actually just step up and do it with no training. . . . That's the equivalent of me walking up to a hospital and saying, 'You

know, I've watched "Grey's Anatomy," so I think I can take that appendix out!'"
This elimination of high school graduates who have no advanced training may
seem so unfair to the high school grad, surely, but there is such an enormous pool
of aspiring actors that professionals choose to use crude sieves for their first elimination from the auditioning pool. The neophyte seeking acting work in theater
must always remember that there is a extremely high level of competition for
available jobs.

Theater casting director Arnold Mungioli put it especially well, saying, "I
think actors learn through work, through doing shows, working with good directors, working off good material, working with playwrights on new projects, and
working under the auspices of good artistic directors." For those with limited
experience, training is very important. Mungioli added, "We are always willing
to look at training to see how competitive it makes one. . . . If an actor is not getting the opportunity to work with great material and grow as an actor, we want
to know that they have been working with teachers and working on material
in classes. They have to show on the résumé that they're growing in one way or
another."

Different casting directors have different prejudices about schools. Dino
Ladki, a film, commercial, and TV casting director, likes Northwestern University and the Juilliard School. Geoffrey Johnson, primarily a casting director for
the Broadway theater, likes NYU and Yale, along with Juilliard. West Coast casting
director Julia Flores, who works mostly in theater, adds Carnegie Mellon, UCLA,
Cal Arts, and Pepperdine. The specific recommendations of individual casting
directors are less important here than their shared commitment to the importance of training beyond high school and undergraduate university.

At the heart of this emphasis on training after high school is the idea of professionalism. Professionals are devoted to their craft. One can become a professional through successful work for pay without education—experience trumps
everything—but in theater, getting the initial jobs for pay is challenging without
training beyond high school.

The Best Advice in This Book

We advise all high school graduates interested in a career in theater to finish
additional training before seeking work. As *Theater Careers* continues, we'll offer
additional reasons besides the ones offered earlier. Here's a start, though. U.S.
Department of Labor statistics for 2008 show that holders of bachelors of arts
degrees are much less likely to be unemployed than those with only a high school
diploma: 2 percent unemployment for B.A. holders vs. 4.4 percent for high school
diploma holders. In 2009 unemployment rates climbed, but the significant difference between unemployment rates for university graduates and high school
graduates continued at 4.6 percent vs. 9.7 percent. A *New York Times* article two

years later, in January 2011, reported that the jobless rate for university graduates was 4.8 percent when the overall jobless rate in the United States was 7.9
percent. As the recession continued, unemployment rates rose for everyone, but
the difference between those with B.A. degrees and those with just high school
diplomas remained roughly the same.

Annual earnings for holders of B.A.s are higher than earnings for people with
only a high school degree. (Note that this is a correlation between completing a
B.A. and salary but does not demonstrate that receiving a B.A. causes an average
increase in salary. It may as well be that people with superior skills both complete
B.A. degrees and achieve higher salaries.) For men with B.A.s, median annual
earnings were $58,340, but high school graduates' median annual earnings were
$34,700. Women with B.A. degrees earned $39,150 and high school graduates
only $22,360. The College Board Advocacy and Policy Center estimates that on
average a holder of a B.A. will receive enough extra income to break even on
the costs of higher education by the age of thirty-three. A Washington research
group, the Hamilton Project, found that college tuition in recent decades has
delivered an inflation-adjusted annual return of more than 15 percent. Compare
this to common stock, where the historical return is about 7 percent.

Even for jobs that don't require a college degree, degree holders in those jobs
make more than people with only a high school diploma, according to a 2011
study by the Center on Education and the Work Force at Georgetown University.
For example, dishwashers with a high school degree earn on average $19,000
yearly, but dishwashers with four-year college degrees make on average $34,000
yearly.

Charles Morey, the artistic director of the Pioneer Theatre Company in Utah,
said, "The best educated individuals make the best artists, artisans, and managers—not to mention colleagues. Go to a good college or university with a
strong emphasis in the liberal arts." Steve Laugerud, director of career services at
DePauw University in Indiana said, "The market is changing so fast, there may be
careers that exist when a student gets out of college that simply didn't exist when
they started."

People working in theater tend to have university degrees. According to the
U.S. Census Bureau's American Community Survey of 2003–5, the percentage of
workers in theater with a B.A. degree or higher are:

58.6 percent of working actors;
46.2 percent of working designers;
69.3 percent of producers and directors;
83.1 percent of writers and authors.

The exception is found for dancers and choreographers, with only 14.4 percent
holding university degrees. This lower figure for dancers and choreographers

may reflect how young dancers often are when they start work in the profession, in part a result of the physical demands of dancing that require young, flexible bodies. A detailed discussion of the American Community Survey, and its findings and restrictions, is found in chapter 3.

When to Delay Education

There is one exception to the advice of casting agents and other theater professionals to get education beyond high school. When an aspiring performer has some special physical attribute that will diminish with time, they might find success exploiting that trait right out of high school. The one quality that comes to mind is being small in stature and able to pass as younger than the actor's real age. Hiring underage performers is very expensive for commercial producers and not-for-profit theaters. Thus the talented adult actor who can look younger can sometimes find work in the professional theater. In touring productions, child actors require tutors. They typically need supervisors, often called *child wranglers*. Child labor laws limit the hours they can rehearse and perform in a week, so major roles may have to be double cast. And adolescents quickly grow up—their voices crack, the boys' beards start to grow, the girls' breasts start to show, and both sexes get that growth-spurt. In a long-running show, replacements must be scouted, cast, and rehearsed continually.

For the musical *Billy Elliot*, playing in London, New York, and on tour, there are three boys cast in the title part for each production. They are not expected to serve more than six months at a stretch. "Basically we are looking for six Billies a year," said *Billy Elliot* casting director Jessica Ronane about the casting needs of the London production. "We always knew that the success of *Billy Elliot* would depend heavily on the child playing Billy, but once it had opened it became evident that the show could not function without an amazing child at its centre." Usually there are twelve potential Billies aged ten to eleven being groomed for the West End alone. They have local dance classes after school and on Saturdays travel to special training. Finding and training Billy Elliots is expensive, but the producer, director, and choreographer determined that casting the role with a truly young man was essential to the story and the effect of the production on the audience. Casting a short nineteen-year-old wouldn't do, although in other circumstances it sometimes can.

Some Real-Life Exceptions to Education before a Career
Matthew Broderick

Matthew Broderick is a real-life example of the advantage of looking younger than one's age, at least in his early career. Broderick is a successful stage, television, and film actor. He is shorter than average height, which had something to do with the start of his career. Matthew Broderick was nineteen when he appeared in the role of David in the last part of Harvey Fierstein's *Torch Song Trilogy* off-Broadway in 1981. David is described in the playscript as fifteen years old. Prior to *Torch Song*, Broderick had a small part in an acting school production of a play by Horton Foote. He was cast in this studio production, at least in part, because his father was in the show and was a friend of Foote. Broderick graduated from Walden School, a now-defunct private high school said to have had a strong drama program. He had no post-secondary-school training. (Secondary school refers to middle school and high school taken together, usually grades six or seven through twelve.) *Torch Song Trilogy* was a cult success until someone convinced the *New York Times'* second-string reviewer, Mel Gussow, to see the production. His rave, including praise for Broderick's performance, gave the show financial success.

Later, Broderick said, "Before I knew it, I was like this guy in a hot play. And suddenly, all these doors opened. And it's only because Mel Gussow happened to come by right before it closed and happened to like it. It's just amazing. All these things have to line up that are out of your control." Broderick recognized the element of luck that boosted his career.

Then he played Eugene Morris Jerome on Broadway in Neil Simon's *Brighton Beach Memoirs* and *Biloxi Blues*. In the first play, Eugene is stated to be fifteen years old. Broderick's first hit-film role was as a high school student interested in computers in 1983's thriller *WarGames* when he was twenty-one. His well-remembered film comedy, *Ferris Bueller's Day Off*, was released in 1986, when Broderick was twenty-four years old. He played the title character, a high school senior.

Sarah Jessica Parker

His wife, Sarah Jessica Parker, is also shorter than average. Her first major role was the eponymous character in *Annie* on Broadway, which she first understudied and then played for a year beginning in 1979, when she was fourteen years old. Annie is described as eleven. Parker had a well-received supporting role as the new girl in a Catholic high school in the film *Footloose* when she was nineteen and played a teenager again in *Girls Just Want to Have Fun* in 1985, when she was twenty. She has no post-secondary-school training, but she did have experience as a child actor and had studied singing and ballet as a child. Her first Broadway role—in 1976, when she was eleven—was in a revival of William Archibald's *The Innocents*, an adaptation of Henry James's ghost novel *The Turn of the Screw*. The production was directed by Harold Pinter, the distinguished English playwright, and starred Claire Bloom, a highly revered actress of her generation, but it ran only twelve performances. Unlike her husband's first experience, Parker's was not in a successful show, despite being directed by a renowned playwright and sharing the stage with an experienced and esteemed actress.

In sum, talented and determined actors are encouraged to attempt to make a career in theater directly out of high school *only* if they have some special physical attribute that will spoil with time. As Broderick notes in recalling the effect of Mel Gussow's serendipitous review of *Torch Song Trilogy*, success always has an aspect of luck involved. And, judging from the biographies of Matthew Broderick and Sarah Jessica Parker, it helps if the young person has a supportive family.

Dropping out of school for a job doesn't always work out.

Noah Robbins

In 2009, Noah Robbins, at the age of nineteen, was accepted to Columbia University, but then was cast as Eugene Jerome in a revival of Neil Simon's *Brighton Beach Memoirs*. Like Matthew Broderick, who originated the role, Robbins is short of stature. Robbins had been to a summer theater camp, performed in school shows, and had professional experience appearing in children's shows at the Kennedy Center. "I was accepted at Columbia a few days before I got this part, so, yeah, it was a good couple of days. But of course, being that it's Columbia, they told me, 'You know, we actually have several other students who are on Broadway right now.' I'm sort of a dime a dozen." Robbins swore before the show opened that he'd earn a B.A. someday. "I'll go when this show is done—and if another amazing thing happens to me, I'll put it off for another year or two." As luck had it, the revival closed November 1, 2009, after only nine performances, probably leaving Robbins enough time to enroll in classes for the spring 2010 term.

Instead he got cast in an off-Broadway premiere, *Secrets of the Trade*, by Jonathan Tolin, which ran in August and September 2010. When Robbins returned to school, he chose to enter Cornell rather than Columbia. He also appeared again on Broadway in the revival of Tom Stoppard's *Arcadia* in the spring of 2011. He played Gus/Augustus, a role said to be younger than sixteen; Robbins was twenty when he undertook the role.

College vs. University

Once there was a fairly useful distinction between the terms *college* and *university*, but that is rapidly fading, as many traditional colleges are renaming themselves universities. One assumes the motive is marketing.

In the United States, a university is a post–secondary school for education and research, which grants academic degrees, both undergraduate and graduate, in a variety of subjects. A university may have organizational units that are called colleges, as well as schools, departments, and units. Many universities offer some professional degrees, such as the L.L.D. (law), M.D. (medical doctor), and D.V.M. (veterinary doctor).

In its traditional meaning, a college referred to an undergraduate institution that offered solely undergraduate degrees in the liberal arts, either the bachelor of arts or bachelor of sciences (B.A. or B.S.).

In *Theater Careers,* when we use the term *university,* it should be read to encompass colleges and universities.

Can Artistry Be Taught?

Professionals in theater and theater education differ about specifics, but most all agree that theater artists benefit from training. Most also agree that both before and after training, there exists some irreducible and hard-to-define innate ability or abilities, generally called *talent.* The extent of the native gift varies among successful artists and the needed capacity varies among theater disciplines. Native talent is developed and enhanced by experience and repetition and a teaching environment is a safe place to get a concentrated dose of experience and repetition. With experience comes freedom, the freedom to concentrate on communication and artistry instead of technique or craft.

A theater designer should have a visual responsiveness and imagination, appreciation for color and line, and probably some capability for drawing. Training enhances these talents and develops technical knowledge of construction methods, materials, and equipment; facility in computer-assisted design and rendering; techniques of scene painting and illusionism; research skills; and historical and literary knowledge.

An actor should have human empathy and psychological insight, a certain exhibitionism, and imagination. Training enhances these talents and develops vocal production and variety, freedom of motion, sensitivity to rhythm and variety, script analysis, and historical and literary knowledge, to name a few helpful qualities.

A playwright must have an active imagination and human empathy, be a storyteller, and be able to work for long periods of time alone. Training develops these gifts and adds knowledge of storytelling forms and historical and literary understanding, and also offers the opportunity to share with other playwrights in training.

The director's talents include to some extent virtually all the talents of the other theater disciplines plus management, assessment, and planning capabilities that come only with training and experience.

All theater artists require a developed work ethic, a commitment to wring the most from the allotted rehearsal time or the allotted budget. High school provides only a limited ability for experience and repetition to develop a student's theater talent. The next step most frequently chosen is getting a bachelor of arts degree.

Bachelor of Arts Degree

Two surveys confirm that the bachelor of arts degree is the one most people hold who work in theater. A survey of off-off-Broadway workers—actors, directors, playwrights, designers, backstage staff—found that 57 percent had bachelors of arts degrees and an additional 28 percent had post-graduate degrees. According to a survey published in 1992 by Columbia University, School of the Arts, about one-half of working actors have a bachelor of arts (B.A.) degree, that is, 45 percent of union actors and 55 percent of nonunion actors. *Dramatics* magazine, the magazine for high school drama students, reported in 2005 that there were 1,352 U.S. theater programs offering the bachelor of arts degree. Clearly the traditional bachelors of arts degree is the certification most often pursued by high school graduates looking to a life in theater (See item ② in fig. 3.)

The B.A. is a liberal arts degree. In this usage, *liberal* doesn't refer to a political slant. The term *liberal arts* has a fine history with varied meanings through time. Starting from medieval times, the liberal arts referred to what a gentleman studied—a man of property who was *liberal,* or at liberty, not servile, and thus free to pursue knowledge for its own sake. Liberal arts study developed a general intellectual ability rather than a technical skill. Classically the subjects were grammar, logic, and rhetoric along with arithmetic, geometry, music, and astronomy and also including the important writers of antiquity; all this comprised preparation for a continuing study of philosophy and, most important, religion.

In the United States today, liberal arts generally refers to post-secondary-school study in humanities, arts and literature, language, and natural and physical sciences at institutions granting the bachelor of arts or bachelor of sciences degrees, depending on the student's area of specialty. Typically liberal arts colleges—sometimes called colleges of science and arts or of science, math, and the arts—require a student to take foundational courses or show capability in areas such as mathematics, English, composition, science, foreign languages, and literature. These courses may be called liberal arts courses, distribution courses, general studies, or the like. In addition the student will have an area of specialization, a major, which will cover one-third to one-half of the student's units of study. For readers of this book the area of specialization would most likely be theater arts. The remaining hours are electives or required survey courses that introduce the student to introductory work in other intellectual disciplines. Many students change majors based on newfound interests discovered in elective or distribution courses. Since undergraduates are usually young and unformed, this introduction to other areas is an important part of a liberal arts education.

We refer solely to a B.A. in theater, but some colleges offer a bachelor of sciences (B.S.) in theater. The primary difference is the terminology. In schools that offer both a B.A. and B.S. in drama, there are usually some differences in the liberal arts or distribution courses between the two degrees, but no difference in total hours or minimum hours required in drama coursework. Also some schools refer to the undergraduate degree as an A.B, initials for the Latin phrase *artium baccalaureus;* again the degrees are not different, just the initials and language.

Many educators argue that a liberal arts degree is less a degree in a subject area than it is a preparation to learn throughout life. *Lifelong learning,* as it's usually called, may be more important than professional study in a single discipline in this era, an era when technology and social organization are rapidly changing. Plus liberal arts education is thought to enrich a person's life outside of work and to make better informed citizens. As Louis Menand, a prominent American writer and Harvard University professor, put it: "Knowledge is a form of capital that is always unevenly distributed, and people who have more knowledge, or greater access to knowledge, enjoy advantages over people who have less. . . . We speak of 'knowledge for its own sake,' but there is nothing we learn that does not put us into a different relation with the world—usually, we hope, a better relation."

A recent study of the effectiveness of undergraduate education, published in 2011 in Richard Arum and Josipa Roksa's *Academically Adrift: Limited Learning on College Campuses,* looked at the generalized ability called *critical thinking.* This study found that undergraduates in traditional liberal arts fields such as social science, humanities, natural science, and mathematics have much higher gains in critical thinking from the university experience than students in practical fields such as business, education, social work, and communications. Critical thinking is a life skill that involves establishing goals, identifying assumptions, looking for hidden values, evaluating evidence, planning and directing actions, and assessing the result.

Requirements for a B.A. Degree

Consider four schools' requirements for a B.A. degree as examples of the *breadth and similarities* among university undergraduate theater programs.

Harvard University

Harvard College, the liberal arts school within Harvard University, defines degree requirements in half-courses, meaning one-semester courses. "Students choose their concentration near the end of their third term in residence. . . . Most concentrations require between 12–14 half-courses, or about 40–45% of a student's overall program." Harvard defines its core curriculum, the courses which can be thought of as electives, as including these areas of study: foreign cultures, historical study, literature and arts, moral reasoning, quantitative reasoning, science, and social analysis. In addition all students must complete a semester of expository writing and show capability in a foreign language.

Incidentally Harvard is unusual but not unique in defining class work as half-courses. Most schools use the term *credit hours,* with "hours" being a measure of convenience, not a measure of actual hours of study. Most one-semester courses will grant three credit hours for successful completion, but some can grant as few as one credit hour. Typically an undergraduate degree is 120 credit hours, or about 35 to 40 one-semester courses.

University of Iowa

The University of Iowa's College of Liberal Arts and Sciences offers a B.A. in Theatre Arts that requires at least seven courses, a total of 21 semester hours, in a set theater curriculum, plus some work on crew for productions and additional theater electives of at least 33 hours total but no more than 50 (about 11 to 18 courses). General studies courses fulfill a liberal arts requirement, with courses in rhetoric, foreign language, interpretation of literature, historical perspectives, humanities, natural sciences, quantitative or formal reasoning, and social sciences. Add electives of the students' choosing, and the degree requires a minimum of 120 hours.

Kenyon College

The small and prestigious Kenyon College in Ohio offers a bachelor of arts with a major in theater that resembles programs elsewhere but with the addition of greater freedom and responsibility. Kenyon defines courses in units. Required theater courses for the major total 5.5 units, plus each student "designs a senior project, a major piece of creative or scholarly work. The student will initiate the work and collaborate with others to see it through to completion." Seniors also must pass a six-hour exam. A normal course load is 4 to 5 units a year with 16 successful units for graduation. Each semester, the student must be enrolled in at least one-half unit from two different departments. This encourages the distribution requirements of a liberal arts degree without requiring specific courses. Or a student in the honors program, with the collaboration of faculty, may construct a personalized "synoptic degree," one that cuts "across departmental and disciplinary boundaries."

University of California, Los Angeles

Most undergraduate theater degrees are awarded by liberal arts colleges, but not all. For example, at the University of California, Los Angeles (UCLA), the School of Theatre, Film, and Television awards a B.A. in theater, not UCLA's College of Letters and Sciences, its liberal arts unit. Yet the degree still covers a liberal arts curriculum with a liberal arts philosophy. "The Bachelor of Arts degree in Theater [from UCLA] provides a liberal arts education and pre-professional training in a comprehensive program that uniquely combines the study of the arts, humanities and sciences with exploration of the principle areas of theater practice. The program is designed to insure that students graduate with a sound humanistic and experiential base for further pursuits in education and in life beyond the university." *Humanistic* in this usage is a synonym for liberal arts. Although the School of Theatre, Film, and Television awards the degree, the B.A. from UCLA is essentially a liberal arts degree.

Liberal Arts Programs vs. Vocational and Professional Degree Programs

Liberal arts degree programs can be contrasted with the vocational and professional degree programs, which include the bachelor of business administration, bachelor of engineering or bachelor of science in engineering, bachelor of science in computer science, bachelor of arts in journalism, bachelor of arts in music or bachelor of music, bachelor degree in information science or librarianship, bachelor of science in nursing, bachelor of science in public health, or bachelor in social work. These degrees are typically granted by university units other than the liberal arts college, such as the School of Nursing or the School of Music. Most of these programs will include some liberal arts components as requirements for the degree, often referred to as humanities courses, cultural enrichment courses, and/or general education courses. Professional degrees are sometimes considered appropriate entry-level degrees for work in the respective discipline.

According to the National Center for Education Statistics, the most often awarded undergraduate degree in recent years has been in business:

> In 2006–07, of the 1.5 million bachelor's degrees awarded that year, over 50 percent were concentrated in five fields: business (21 percent); social sciences and history (11 percent); education (7 percent); health professions and related clinical sciences (7 percent); and psychology (6 percent). During the same time period, the fields of visual and performing arts (6 percent), engineering and engineering technologies (5 percent),communication and communications technologies (5 percent), and biological and biomedical sciences (5 percent) represented about an additional 20 percent of all bachelor's degrees awarded.

A bachelor's degree in theater would be included in the 6 percent of degrees awarded in the fields of visual and performing arts.

The B.A. degree is a prerequisite for pursuing graduate degrees from among the M.F.A., the M.A./Ph.D. series, or the M.A.T. for teachers. (See item ④, ⑤, and ⑥, respectively, in fig. 3.) The B.A. is also a prerequisite for pursuing a number of advanced professional degrees, such as a law degree or a master of business administration (M.B.A.). In those cases, typically the area of concentration of the B.A. is not important in pursuing the professional degree, just grade averages and scores on graduate school entry exams. The B.A. is a required degree in many cases for any number of entry-level positions in much of the work force.

Bachelors of Fine Arts Degree

The bachelors of fine arts degree (B.F.A.) in theater is an alternative to the B.A. degree for high school graduates (See item ③ in fig. 3). The B.F.A. is offered mostly by four-year colleges and universities. The B.F.A. is sometimes considered final preparation to enter a profession and so is referred to, along with the master of fine arts (M.F.A.) and the doctor of philosophy (Ph.D.), as a *terminal degree*. Fine arts degrees are not preparation for postgraduate education because the coursework is focused on forming a professional to work in the field. (Some graduate schools will recognize the B.F.A. as preparation for the M.F.A., but many do not.) A B.F.A. or an M.F.A. is not considered prerequisite to the M.A. or Ph.D. degrees. To differentiate the undergraduate theater degrees further, most theater B.A. programs are general concentrations in theater, although students may choose to concentrate their electives on one area. Most B.F.A. programs are focused on one area of specialty in theater, such as production design and technology, playwriting, stage management, or theater performance. (These specific areas of B.F.A. concentration are from Ohio University, School of Theatre, but these specializations are typical of many college B.F.A. programs.)

B.F.A. programs typically require two-thirds of class hours in the arts including studio work and other practical courses, with one-third in general studies. Whereas in most universities, an enrolled undergraduate can declare a major such as theater without further admission requirements, most B.F.A. programs require an audition or portfolio review for admittance.

According to the theater accrediting body, the National Association of Schools of Theatre (NAST), a B.F.A. places "primary emphasis . . . on the development of skills, concepts, and sensitivities essential to the theatre professional." Contrast this with NAST's description of the B.A. as providing a broad range of knowledge in the arts, humanities, and sciences as well as theater.

The B.F.A. is not as widely offered as the B.A. degree. Definitive figures are not available, but we have summarized the directory of post-secondary-school educational programs published in *Back Stage* in the spring of 2011. The B.A. degree was offered by 397 of the programs listed; the B.F.A. was offered by 154 programs. All but 35 of the B.F.A.-granting institutions also grant a B.A. in theater.

For an example of a B.F.A. program, consider that of Ohio University. All B.F.A. undergraduates take 18 hours of introductory courses that include introduction to performance, design, stage construction, play analysis, directing, and three courses in theater history. In addition the general undergraduate requirements for the college must be met, which include demonstrating competency in English composition and completing 32 hours in distribution classes, classes from a breadth of intellectual disciplines outside of theater. For the B.F.A. in production design and technology, another 43 hours are required, with intermediate and advanced courses in stagecraft and design skills, and some coursework in the history of art, costumes, or furniture and interior design, plus 15 hours of electives in the area of specialization. For the B.F.A. in performance, studio performance courses are the core of the program, with a different focus each year of the three-year program. Ohio University also offers the B.F.A. in playwriting and in stage management. Note that individual schools differ in what constitutes a B.F.A. degree, with some requiring little general liberal arts courses while focusing intensely on theater coursework and production work and with others requiring more liberal arts study.

Associate in/of Arts Degree

The associate in/of arts degree (A.A.) is generally a two-year degree although students requiring remedial classes may take more study to complete the program. (See item ⑦ in fig. 3.) The greatest number of A.A. degrees are granted by community colleges or junior colleges, but some four-year colleges and universities have A.A.-granting programs in addition to their four-year degrees. Some independent schools of theater, proprietary (for-profit) and not-for-profit, grant the A.A. degree. Judging from the programs listed in *Back Stage's* directory of post-secondary schools, the A.A. as a theater degree is not common: only 15 were listed, out of a total of 447 degree-granting institutions.

In general the A.A. degree comes in two types, transfer and vocational. The transfer degree is taken by students who hope to transfer to a bachelor of arts program at a four-year school or whose high school grades would not get them admitted to the four-year university of their choice. Two-year schools are usually less expensive than four-year schools per year or per credit hour. Additionally many community college students enroll part-time or take night classes after work; part-time enrollment is generally more difficult to do at a four-year school since limited courses are offered at night and on weekends. Transfer degrees usually have general education courses such as English composition, algebra, humanities, and the like, as well as specific work in the area of specialization. A vocational degree is preparation for a career. Some jobs may require at least A.A. degrees, including positions for dental hygienist, physical therapy assistant, paralegal, and electronics technician. Some schools offer A.A. degrees in acting or drama as vocational degrees.

Non-Degree-Granting Schools

One choice open to high school graduates is to train at a non-degree-granting institution. (See item ⑧ in fig. 3.) Typically these schools train only actors. Some are not-for-profit and some proprietary, or for-profit. Some are affiliated with a regional theater, and others spring from the acting instruction of a founder, a "guru" to the actors he or she has taught. Some have set curricula with a certificate granted on completion of the course of study or when two year's work has been concluded. The certificate has no traditional standing among academics, as do the associate of arts and bachelor of arts. What the certificate qualifies the completing student to do next is impossible to say. Generally there is no federal financial support for students at these non-degree-granting schools.

Many of these non-degree-granting schools are in New York City or the Los Angeles area. For example, the *Back Stage* directory of New York acting schools and coaches in spring 2011 listed 175 vendors in acting technique and scene study.

Without implying any recommendation of the schools mentioned, the following are some examples. The examples suggest the breadth and similarity among non-degree-granting theater training institutions.

What Does Conservatory *Mean?*

Some writers refer to all actor training sources that are not traditional colleges or universities as conservatories. The problem with the term is that it is not consistently used. Florida State University runs an M.F.A. program called the Asolo Conservatory for Actor Training. Baltimore Actors' Theatre runs the Conservatory, which it calls a college preparatory school of the arts for grades pre-one through twelve. The Actors' Conservatory Theatre in San Diego is a theater company for young people, not a training program at all. For this reason we choose not to use the word *conservatory* to mean non-degree-granting schools.

The Neighborhood Playhouse

The Neighborhood Playhouse started with the legendary acting teacher Sanford Meisner, who was one of the founders of the Group Theatre. Meisner's successful students include James Caan, Steve McQueen, Robert Duvall, Gregory Peck, Bob Fosse, Diane Keaton, Peter Falk, Jon Voight, Jeff Goldblum, Tony Randall, and Sydney Pollack. (Note that the youngest of these is Goldblum, born in 1952. Meisner died in 1997 at the age of 92.) "The Neighborhood Playhouse School of the Theatre provides a full-time conservatory atmosphere that concentrates on the artistic growth of the actor through a fusion of technical training in acting, movement, speech, voice and singing combined with a deeper understanding of the cultural values underlying a life devoted to the highest and most demanding artistic principles." Tuition is $11,180 yearly. It has about seventy students. It offers no degrees but does give a certificate of completion after two years work. Its two full-time and fifteen part-time teachers include five who hold M.A.s or M.F.A.s, and twelve without advanced degrees. It admits about one-half of applicants.

PCPA Theaterfest

PCPA Theaterfest, in Santa Maria, California, awards a certificate in acting after two years study. "The class schedule is rigorous; blending studio classes, lectures, labs, rehearsals and performance experiences. The program is unique in that in addition to studios, labs and classes, students receive mentorship from professional artists; in the studio, in one-on-one tutorials and in the context of producing PCPA (Pacific Conservatory of the Performing Arts) Theaterfest's professional Actors' Equity Association productions." Theaterfest has three full-time faculty and twenty-eight part-time faculty, including one Ph.D., 22 M.A.s or M.F.A.s, and eight teachers without advanced degrees. Theaterfest states that some students transfer to B.F.A. programs with more than 70 units of transferable credit. It accepts 45 of 500 applicants.

National Conservatory of Dramatic Arts

Located in Washington, D.C., the National Conservatory of Dramatic Arts grants a diploma in acting. Its curriculum is based on the teachings of Michel Saint-Denis, who "emphasized that a school is not only a place to learn from the past but a place to explore new ideas and experiment in ways not possible in commercial theatre." Born in France, Saint-Denis, at the age of thirty-eight, founded, with others, the London Theatre Studio in 1935, an actor-training institution that is still practicing today. He worked at the Old Vic and the Royal Shakespeare Company and was an early teacher at New York's Juilliard School. He died in 1971. The twelve full-time and six part-time teachers include two Ph.D.s and six M.A.s or M.F.A.s. The conservatory awards a diploma in acting and an advanced certificate in acting for students who remain for a third year of study, and it admits two out of every three applicants. It operates a sixty-seat black box theater space, that is, a space not originally designed to be a theater, generally with no space to fly scenery and with seating for the audience on movable risers that let the acting area be reconfigured for each show. Typically the rooms are painted flat-black everywhere to control light reflection, hence the name "black box."

M.F.A. Degrees

The master of fine arts degree (M.F.A.) is a postgraduate degree for holders of the B.A. (and in some institutions the B.F.A.) to receive intensive training in their discipline, intended to prepare the student for a career in the field. (See item ④ in fig. 3.) In addition some two-year schools and some universities will engage M.F.A. holders as teachers.

Most M.F.A. programs are intended to be completed in two or three years and include some period of internship in a working, professional theater. NAST accreditation standards are that an M.F.A. degree be at least sixty or ninety credit hours. This is about double the hours required for a M.A. degree. In M.F.A. programs, there is an emphasis on a mix of classroom study and practical experience in finished theater presentations, as actors, designers, and other positions. Areas of specialization might include theater administration, acting, scenic design, lighting design, costume design, playwriting, dramaturgy, or stage management. Some programs offer only acting or acting and directing as specialty areas. To enter an M.F.A. program almost always requires auditions, interviews, and/or portfolio reviews. On completion the students are declared ready to work professionally in their chosen fields.

The National Office for Arts Accreditation, an organization made up of the four accrediting bodies for higher education in the arts—theater, dance, music, and art and design—defines minimum student outcomes for the M.F.A.

To graduate with an M.F.A., students must

- Demonstrate professional competence in one or more aspects of the creation and presentation of works of art and design, dance, or theatre.
- Produce creative and academic work that shows the ability to integrate knowledge and skills in their field and other areas of inquiry and research.
- Complete graduate-level studies associated with their discipline in areas such as history, critical analysis, aesthetics, methodologies, and related humanities, sciences, and social sciences.
- Produce a major final project demonstrating mastery in their field or area of specialization.

Scott L. Steele, executive director of the University/Resident Theatre Association (U/RTA) stated that "graduate training effectively provides the network of contemporary colleagues, as well as of accomplished professionals encountered during that training, which will, more than anything else, help a young professional to first gain work."

Without implying a recommendation, the following offers some examples of the range of M.F.A. curricula available. These programs, from varied parts of the country, suggest some of the range of approaches to M.F.A. programs.

The University of San Diego

The University of San Diego, working with the NFP Old Globe Theatre in San Diego, offers an M.F.A. in acting. Students complete sixty units of graduate work in two years. The goal, as stated in the school's catalog, is for the student to "demonstrate the ability to integrate the fundamentals of Stanislavski's psychological/physical technique of action with the demands of playing texts of heightened

language; exhibit proficiency in combining full breath support, rich vocal reso-
nation and articulation precision when speaking texts for the stage; demonstrate
skill in analyzing and interpreting dramatic texts, researching literary sources
and referencing stage history as fundamental tools in preparing for performance,
and demonstrate a variety of physical techniques in order to transform the body
into a creative resource for the exploration of text, character and relationships."

Wayne State University

Wayne State University in Detroit through its College of Fine, Performing, and
Communication Arts offers a theater M.F.A. in six areas of specialization. The
course work is interwoven with production in the school's two theaters. For
actors morning classes include

> acting, voice and movement. Acting classes emphasize the exploration of
> various techniques, including neutral mask, physical action, playing goals
> and obstacles, study of verse, scansion and characterization. Movement
> classes emphasize alignment, agility and strength as well as period dance/
> deportment and Pilates-based body conditioning by a certified instructor
> in the Pilates method of body conditioning. Voice classes emphasize Patsy
> Rodenburg's approach to vocal workout and heightened text, working to
> ground the student in language through the words, thought structures and
> images. The department invites guest artists and teachers for additional
> instruction in movement, dance, Shakespearean play analysis and perfor-
> mance, audition technique, and the "business" side of acting.

In the afternoons, the actors rehearse for the season of plays offered by the school.
For those specializing in costume design, "the typical course of study includes
traditional courses in design technique and technical production. . . . learn[ing]
the techniques of costume technology through production work with plays of
many genres, periods and styles."

Yale University

Within Yale University, the Yale School of Drama offers the M.F.A. in nine specialty areas of study. According to its catalog, Yale's M.F.A. in playwriting is
"designed to guide the writer in finding strategies, honest and astonishing, that
articulate the personal and cultural impulses for writing and making theatre.
. . . The playwright creatively and critically employs character recipes, narrative
strategies, organizing principles of form, poetic images, political and aesthetic
manifestos, sinewy language, and the plasticity of the stage to convey and challenge our private and public dreams. The goal of the department is to encourage
the widest range of work possible, in a variety of mediums, and to mentor each
playwright's evolving understanding and translation of their voice." For theater

management specialty, Yale "prepares aspiring leaders to create organizational environments increasingly favorable to the creation of theatre art and its presentation to appreciative audiences. The department provides students with the knowledge, skills, experience, and values to enter the field at high levels of responsibility, to move quickly to leadership positions, and ultimately to advance the state of management practice and the art form itself."

M.A./Ph.D. Degrees

The Master of Arts (M.A.) degree is traditionally considered as the first step in pursuing the Doctor of Philosophy (Ph.D.) degree. (See item ⑤ in fig. 3.) However, public school teachers may also pursue the M.A. degree in pursuit of pay upgrades. These degrees are intensive study in one discipline and practice in conducting research in the field. The research for the Ph.D. in particular should be original, adding to the sum of knowledge in the field, and the Ph.D. dissertation, which accounts for that research, should be declared publishable by a committee of peers. At one time some schools required the Ph.D. dissertation to be published, but this is rare today. The Ph.D. should be seen as the prerequisite for teaching and research at a university. Some theater Ph.D. holders with university positions continue to work as professionals in their fields, as actors, directors, designers, and playwrights. In the current economic environment and the current budgeting environment for higher education, many with a Ph.D. find work other than in a college or university.

Some universities also offer a doctor of arts (D.A.) degree in a very few disciplines. The difference between a Ph.D. and a D.A. degree is that the Ph.D. emphasizes research and publication while the D.A. emphasizes practicing the discipline. A school of music, for example, may grant a Ph.D. in musicology or music history for the student intending to do original research in those fields and also a D.A. in composition, performance, or other areas for the practicing or teaching musician. Yale School of Drama offers a doctor of fine arts degree (D.F.A.) in dramaturgy and dramatic criticism, but as an earned degree the Yale D.F.A. is unique in the United States. The D.F.A. is commonly an *honorary* degree granted to individuals who have had made notable contributions working in their artistic field.

Professional Science Masters Degrees

Universities have begun to offer master's degrees that are not part of the M.A./ Ph.D. traditional approach but rather are considered professional degrees. Sometimes called a "professional science master," or P.S.M., they are offered in areas that include clinical psychology, automotive design, divinity, public history, nursing, strategic communication, and preservation and presentation of the moving image. Often P.S.M. degrees are keyed to local industries. Thus in Florida a P.S.M. is offered in simulation. Think Disney.

This change reflects needs for more specific jobs-oriented training. According to some education professionals, the growth of P.S.M. degrees shows a downgrading by human resources departments of the value of a B.A.

In theater and in other arts, the M.F.A. serves the same function as the P.S.M. but has a longer history.

The Education Paths in Brief

High school graduates who want more study in theater have a number of alternatives. They may pursue a bachelor of arts degree, a bachelor of fine arts degree, an associate in arts degree, or may study in a non-degree-granting school. People with an A.A. degree may work in the field or transfer credits to a four-year university to complete a B.F.A. or B.A. degree. Recipients of the B.F.A. degree may pursue work in their field or get advanced training through an M.F.A. degree. Holders of a B.A. in theater may work in theater or pursue additional study, working toward an M.F.A. degree if their primary goal is to work in the professional theater. If they prefer to teach, they can pursue the master of arts in teaching (M.A.T.) degree or the M.A./Ph.D. degrees, for teaching at the public school or university level, respectively. All these paths are summarized in fig. 3.

Beyond the Facts

The advantages of an education beyond high school of at least a bachelor of arts degree are clear. On average, people with a B.A. earn more money throughout their working lives and are less likely to be unemployed.

Education beyond the high school diploma is viewed by many theater professionals as an entry ticket to *consideration* for available work. Theater professionals infer that this education shows seriousness about becoming a professional. Producers, artistic directors, and casting directors who are looking to entrust a show to a director, designer, actor, and others consider education credentials because school is a safe place to practice, practice, practice one's craft—failing at times but learning artistry along the way.

The highest degree for theater artists is the M.F.A., which is often a three-year training program following a B.A. and includes an internship in a working professional theater to introduce the student to the profession.

The main reason to pursue the M.A./Ph.D. path is to teach at a college or university. The plum university teaching positions—those with tenure—are few, however, and the competition intense. This struggle has accelerated during the past decade so that now the majority of university teaching jobs are low-paying adjunct positions or filled by even lower-paid graduate students.

Beyond the facts lie opinions. Here are some of ours. Earning a degree should not be the only goal of those who enter university. Getting only a paper degree from university is not enough payback for the time and money invested. If a student is satisfied with doing the minimum, then this student will get only the minimum a university has to offer.

We urge college students to take advantage of all opportunities. Those who want to be actors, playwrights, or directors are encouraged to crew as many shows as they possibly can. (If nothing else, they will learn to use power tools safely.) Those who want to be designers should do the same, of course, and most programs will require them to do so. The opportunity to practice, practice, *practice* theater is an essential component of a meaningful university theater education. Actors with two-line and even no-line parts can still learn at rehearsals, by being involved in what's happening among the other actors and between the director and other artists. Student designers who assist a faculty designer will learn in the theater and the scene shop as well as in the classroom. Especially they will learn the difference between ideal solutions and good solutions that fit time and budget.

All future theater artists should see as much theater as possible, even if the production isn't of professional quality. Seeing less than stellar work and asking oneself, "How could I have improved this production?," can provide great insight. In addition, we advise

> Get involved as an artist and as an audience member at student-run theater. To make a baseball analogy, student-run theater is "batting practice" for the future professional. Take any opportunity to stand up and swing.
> Read plays; many can be gulped down in under two hours. Always carry one with you.
> Keep current with your planned profession by following professional magazines and journals. See chapter 7, "Getting Your Own Facts," for specific information on this subject.
> Usher for a local presenter of Broadway-style tours to see the professionals and avoid the high ticket prices.
> Usher at dance and opera performances to learn more about rhythm, lighting, and design.
> Find a set of friends who are as driven to be theater artists as you are. Avoid the slackers.
> Volunteer to review theater for the school newspaper or the local free paper; refining one's impressions and opinions by writing focuses the mind and starts the process of developing taste.

Changing one's major in response to the experience of other disciplines coming from distribution/liberal arts courses is not a sign of weakness . Rather it is a sign of courage and open-mindedness. The opportunity for a lucky intellectual discovery is part of the reason universities require liberal arts courses outside of the student's chosen major.

CHAPTER 3

Choosing a University—Consider Time and Money

The choice of which educational path to follow affects the time and money that will be consumed in education. But the commonly discussed plan and budget for the time and money to a degree is often not reflected by reality. Many of the short-cut tools to college evaluation, especially national ranking systems, are probably of little value in choosing a school.

Time to a B.A.

The curriculum plan of most universities is that an undergraduate degree be completed in four years. But the standard for comparing undergraduate schools is the percent of freshmen who complete the bachelor degree in six years. On average in the United States, only about one-half of freshmen will obtain a bachelor degree within six years of enrollment. Schools differ greatly in the percentage of freshmen who complete the B.A. degree in six years. Harvard University graduates about 98 percent within six years. Only 33 percent of the freshmen entering the University of Massachusetts Boston graduate in six years. For commercial for-profit schools, the percentages are even smaller. The commercial University of Phoenix graduates only 9 percent of new students within six years.

Net Cost of a B.A. Degree, Not List Price

Newspaper and magazine accounts of the cost of a B.A. degree usually state the published figures provided by the universities, the list price. A better, more meaningful way to look at university expenses is net costs. For tuition this means subtracting grants and scholarships to derive the net tuition. For some expenses, such as room and board, in order to derive net costs the cost of going to university must be compared to the cost of not going to university and staying in the workforce. There are also lost wages, the money the young people might have earned if, instead of going to university, they went to work.

Net Tuition

The average yearly tuition for an undergraduate degree is $25,143 per year at a private university and $6,585 at a public university, according to 2008–9 reports. These prices do not include room and board. These tuition figures are the average list price, but many students pay less than list price. The average net price of federal and state government grants is much lower for those students qualifying for the grants. Average *net* tuition at an in-state four-year public school is $2,000 and at a private university $11,900. Add to this the cost of textbooks, estimated to be as much as $1,000 per year.

As a result of the Higher Education Opportunity Act of 2008, the U.S. Department of Education has published an online database of university tuitions, net tuition, and rates of inflation in tuition. Called the "Higher Education Opportunity Act Information of College Costs," it can be found at http://collegecost.ed.gov/.

Incremental Room and Board

Most journalists writing about university costs include the cost of room and board as part of the cost of higher education. However, everyone has a room and board cost, student or not. It's a basic cost of living.

If parents provide housing for a high school graduate not going to university, then the young person would not incur the cost of room and board. The parents still have those costs. Otherwise parents could move to smaller quarters; some do just that, especially after the last child leaves home. They could convert their child's room into some other use—say, an office or craft room—and get utility from the space if no savings. If the child staying at home after high school doesn't reimburse his parents for board—meals and such—the family still incurs those costs. Newspapers and magazines report that many young people, even those with B.A. degrees, are still living with their parents. The reports don't say whether the parents like that arrangement. Most young people would probably choose to live away from their parents, for social reasons if nothing else.

The question remains, what is the *extra* room and board for going to university versus not going to university? It is generally agreed that the cost of housing in a university community is higher than elsewhere for similar levels of quality, but the average premium for living near a university is unknown. For most purposes it is probably too small an amount to matter.

Lost Wages

An additional cost—from an economist's point of view an *opportunity cost*—is the student's reduced ability to earn money. If not enrolled, the youngsters—one hopes—could find full-time work. The lost wages, or opportunity cost, is the difference between the amount of money that is earnable as a student as opposed to what could be earned if not going to school and working full-time.

Consider a freshman who works ten hours a week while going to school. Because being a student is itself a full-time job, this person is not earning money the additional thirty hours per week (assuming a forty-hour work week) during the nine months of school. At the federal minimum wage of $7.25 per hour, the lost wages would be $7,830 per year (thirty hours per week x four weeks per month x nine months per year as a student x the minimum wage). In this hypothetical example, the opportunity cost of lost wages is greater than the average net cost of tuition at a public university, or $7,830 lost wages vs. $2,000 average net tuition. At an in-state public university, the student's lost wages may be the greatest net cost of attending school.

Graduating with Student Loans Is Not Universal

Despite the high costs of postsecondary education, a 2009 report from the College Board says only 66 percent of graduates from four-year public colleges accumulated some debt. The median level of debt for some with a bachelor's degree who borrowed money was $17,700 in 2007–8. However, students do undertake forms of debt *other than* student loans. Average credit card debt for B.A. graduates is more than $4,000.

In comparing student loans with credit card debt, there are two opposing facts. The interest on credit card debt is much higher than for student loans. Credit cards are unsecured debt, and college students usually have no credit history. It would not be surprising if student credit card interest rates exceed 21 percent a year. Student loans, by contrast, had interest rates in the 8 to 10 percent range as of summer 2011. However, credit card debt can be excused in bankruptcy; student loan debt is virtually never excused in bankruptcy. This difference in bankruptcy rules is one reason credit card debt is so much more expensive than student loans. Of course, no one plans to go through bankruptcy, but bankruptcy happens to many good people.

Time to Completion of Graduate Degrees
M.F.A.

Depending on the school, an M.F.A. is intended to be completed in two or three years. Statistics on the rate of completion for the M.F.A. are limited. One small sample of recipients of a specific federal fellowship for "students of superior academic ability" found only 51 percent of these students completed of the M.F.A. within seven years. These were M.F.A. degrees in *any* arts discipline, not just theater.

M.A./PH.D.

The coursework for a M.A./Ph.D. degree typically requires at least one to three years of study to complete. Another two to four years are often needed to complete a Ph.D. dissertation, a substantial and original contribution to knowledge, ranging from 50 to 450 pages. The dissertation undergoes faculty review, and the student endures an oral examination, often called a defense of the dissertation. This is the proposed work plan. In reality the average time to a Ph.D. in the humanities is a little more than ten years. The cold fact is that 43 percent of Ph.D. candidates in all disciplines never earn the degree.

Relevant Facts for Choosing a University

It would be great if there were clear and reliable facts to guide the student in choosing a university. Most libraries have gobs of directories of college and university programs, detailing addresses and phone numbers, website addresses, major staff members, enrollment numbers, list-price tuition, and the like. These facts by themselves are not enough to make a choice.

Theater Education Advertising

Many theater programs in universities and non-degree-granting institutions advertise in magazines, sometimes providing just the facts and sometimes offering marketing promises that can be fairly extravagant. See the list below. Is "Discover Your Inner Character!" something that happens in a university theater department or in psychotherapy? Can a state university in the Midwest really claim, "We set the stage for the future of American Theater"? Clearly, relying on advertising promises isn't much help in choosing a theater training program, as the claims quoted below show. The source is *American Theatre*, January 2011.

Do the Marketing Slogans from Theater Education Advertisements Really Mean Anything?

Recruitment Promise	School
1 extraordinary education	UNC School of the Arts
Act like you own the world.	University of Kentucky
Because here, you don't need to compromise.	University of Maryland
Breaking Through . . . to your future!	Bradley University
Create the future you dream	Santa Fe University of Art and Design
Discover Your Inner Character!	Niagara University
Explore, Innovate, and Create the Future of American Theatre	Boston University
Inspiring Passion. Sparking Innovation. Developing Artistry.	Western Michigan University

KNOWS NO BOUNDARIES	Sarah Lawrence
Learn Grow Live Teach Be	Kentucky Shakespeare National Performance & Voice Institute
Master the art of transformation	Actors Movement Studio Conservatory
Nurture your Dreams!	Indiana University
On the vanguard of new and experimental work	University of Texas at Austin
Reach your dreams	University of Northern Colorado
Reaching Falling Standing	Abilene Christian University
Reignite your creative process	Concordia University
Take your training to the next level	Stella Adler Studio of Acting
The acting education of a lifetime . . . for a gifted, passionate few.	New York Conservatory for Dramatic Arts
The Artist's Journey Begins Here	Coastal Carolina University
THE NEXT STAGE, a life-changing theatre education in a world-class institution	Wellesley College
Transforming Lives, One Stage at a Time	Michigan State University
Turn Your Passion into Your Life's Work!	Kean University
Turn Your Passion Into Your Profession	Salisbury University
Waiting for Inspiration?	Florida State
We put the future on stage NOW!	Utah Valley University
We set the stage for the future of American Theater	Northern Illinois University
We will surprise you.	Virginia Tech
Where the emphasis is on you.	University of Tulsa
Why wait to do what you love?	University of Indianapolis

The promises made in some advertisements for theater students are clearly excessive. Perhaps high school seniors are inured to marketing promises because, according to the American Academy of Pediatrics, young people see about forty thousand advertisements a year.

U.S. News & World Report's "America's Best Colleges" and Similar Rankings

At least one newsmagazine attempts to collect, weight, and compile relevant statistics for American universities, publishing a set of rankings of the best universities in the country. *U.S. News & World Report* was a newsmagazine similar to *Time* and *Newsweek*. The magazine published its first "America's Best Colleges" report in 1983 and its rankings remain the most widely quoted evaluation of U.S. schools. Beginning in 2010, the magazine stopped printing weekly hardcopies, becoming an online only journal—*except* for its "Best of . . ." editions, which are still distributed on newsstands. The popularity of the university rankings publication, hard copy and online, is undeniable. For the 2007 release the *U.S. News* website received 10 million page views in three days, compared to half a million views in a typical month. The *U.S. News* college rankings are based on data supplied by each educational institution from an annual survey sent to each school. They are also based on opinion surveys of university faculties and administrators, asked for opinions of schools other than their own. In essence the ranking is based on seven weighted variables, themselves made up of combinations of measures

Undergraduate academic reputation
Graduation and freshmen retention rates
Faculty resources
Student selectivity
Financial resources
Graduation rate performance
Alumni giving

Once the *U.S. News* ranking became influential, it received mounting criticism. Some schools have refused to cooperate. The problems with this ranking, and perhaps any similar ranking, are many. First and foremost it takes measures on very different scales and values and weights and combines them into one rank. It's analogous to ranking friends based on some arithmetical combination of their height plus their hair color plus their grade averages. The resulting ranking of friends based on these mixed criteria would be silly.

The *U.S. News* college rankings give the impression that they're objective, but hidden in the weighting system are value judgments. For example, the *U.S. News* ranking does not consider the cost of tuition *at all* in comparing schools. For most students and parents, the cost of tuition is an essential variable in choosing a university.

Heterogeneous schools are measured against each other. The *U.S. News* ranking, for example, rates large state universities such as the University of Michigan, with an enrollment of more than forty thousand students, against small, private schools such as Yeshiva University, with an enrollment of fewer than 6,500 students. Both are compared by the same measures.

Some schools are known to "game" the rankings, to make decisions to increase their placement on the scale. One rating is for the percent of freshmen applications accepted, arguing that the fewer applications a school accepts, the more selective it is. Some schools have increased their marketing and outreach to increase the numbers of applications submitted to them, with no plan to increase the size of the student body. By rejecting more applications, these schools raised their rankings.

Or some schools just lie. Claremont McKenna College in California admitted in January 2012 that for six years it submitted false SAT scores to rating publications, such as *U.S. News & World Report.* The vice president and dean of admissions resigned because of the scandal. Claremont McKenna is a well-regarded school. What's astounding is that its real median freshman SAT was 1400, a value of which many schools would be very proud. The school reported the score raised by only ten points. This college is not alone. In the fall 2011, Iona Callege, New York, admitted to lying for years on multiple items used in ranking.

And the ranking systems are circular, at least in part. Past highly ranked schools tend to be highly ranked in the future. Every year, the magazine surveys university presidents, provosts, and admissions deans, along with some high school guidance counselors, asking them to grade schools from one to five. Those at national universities were asked in a recent survey to grade 261 other national universities. In truth few of those asked have personal knowledge of a large number of other schools. So they rely on hearsay about the quality of other schools or even on published university rankings, maybe even last year's *U.S. News* list of the best colleges.

U.S. News and World Report university rankings aren't uniquely bad. To some extent, any system that attempts to reduce university performance to a single number will have some or all of the procedural faults of *U.S. News.* This includes the rankings from *Forbes Magazine, Washington Monthly, Fiske Guide to Colleges, Princeton Review,* and many others.

Theater Program Accreditation

Whereas all universities will be accredited, only some theater programs are accredited at the program level. There may be little evidence in favor of a choosing a university whose theater program is accredited. It doesn't deserve a great deal of weight in decision-making.

Accreditation is a process for certifying that an individual or institution meets minimal standards for practice in some field. A hospital must be accredited. The term *certified public accountant* designates one accredited in the field of accountancy. In post-secondary schooling—four-year universities and two-year degree-granting institutions— accreditation is required for eligibility for most federal assistance or grant funds. Many other sources of funds follow the government lead and require accreditation as well. The Higher Education Act of 1965 requires the U.S. secretary of education to publish a list of accrediting agencies determined to be reliable authorities on the quality of education or training provided by institutions of higher education. Except for the secretary's identifying the certification authorities, the federal government has no part in accreditation. Educational accreditation is a peer-review process, coordinated by accreditation commissions that are funded and governed by the collaborating colleges and universities.

There are regional and national accrediting bodies for colleges and universities, with the regional bodies accrediting not-for-profit institutions and the national bodies accrediting proprietary ones. The regional bodies are called *associations* and include the Southern Association of Colleges and Schools (SACS), the New England Association of Schools and Colleges (NEASC), and others. Virtually all colleges and universities are accredited by an established authority because of the requirement for accreditation for many forms of financial assistance. Thus university-level accreditation is uniform and does not contain information that can be used to choose one among a number of schools.

In addition individual areas of study may *choose* to be accredited by specialized associations. For theater the accrediting body is the National Association of Schools of Theatre (NAST). There are about 160 theater programs accredited by NAST. According to NAST, "Typically, the accreditation process includes 1) a self-evaluative description (self-study) of the institution or unit, 2) an on-site review by a team of evaluators, and 3) judgment by an accreditation decision-making body, normally called a Commission. Accreditation reviews focus on educational quality, institutional integrity, faculty credentials, and educational improvements."

Accreditation is a time-consuming process for the individual school and is not undertaken lightly. Despite NAST claims accreditation is not a measure of the *quality* of a theater program, rather it is a measure of *minimum capabilities* of a program in terms of policies, faculty credentials, physical facilities, and the like. Only about 10 percent of theater departments in the United States that offer the B.A. are NAST accredited. It is interesting to note that a number of the most highly regarded university theater programs in the country are not members of NAST. Among the programs that are *not* accredited are those at Yale, Carnegie-Mellon, Juilliard, NYU/Tisch School of the Arts, UCLA, and others. Since departmental accreditation does not affect financial support, it remains primarily a marketing tool for member institutions. The most highly regarded programs apparently do not need the marketing support of NAST membership. In addition to handling college and university theater programs, NAST also accredits non-degree-granting schools.

Gathering Many Facts to Choose a University

Choosing a university is never going to be reducible to a single calculation, number, or fact. Nor is there a meaningful way to examine all the thousands of drama programs in the United States. Neither of these conclusions means that gathering some information won't help young people and their parents make better choices. The following is a synopsis of what a number of experts in the field say can be important in evaluating university theater programs.

> Tuition costs and likelihood of financial aid, focusing on *net* tuition costs
> How many and what type of shows the theater department stages—
>   musicals, mainstream plays, avant-garde, and political work
> Student-centered or "laboratory" production programs
> Faculty training and professional experience in the field
> Placement of graduates in jobs and graduate schools
> Size of the university and size of the community
> Geographic distance from family
> Racial and gender makeup of student body

The individual student will decide what is important. Some students want a big university with tens of thousands of students; some think they can thrive better in a small college. Some want to stay in close proximity to their homes; others want to try to live more independently, far from home. This is another reason why published rankings are hard to apply to the individual student.

Many sources recommend using published directories, which are available in many public and school libraries to narrow choices. Having settled on a few possibilities, prospective students can visit schools to gather more information than directories offer by talking with some faculty and students, auditing some courses, seeing some shows, eating in the dining hall, and the like.

Beyond the Facts

Earning a B.A. degree is expensive. Many newspaper and magazine accounts of the costs of a university degree, however, exaggerate the costs by disclosing the average list-price costs, not the *net price* of an undergraduate degree. Despite what one might read in periodicals, it is possible that a B.A. degree can be completed *without taking on student loans*. At one selective college, students reported defining the purpose of student loans not just as an investment in the future but also as a means to experience fully the college life, which they characterized as frequent socializing, travel, and entertainment. This is a frivolous attitude when taking on debt that one will repay for a very long time.

Whatever the costs, it is now clear that universities differ greatly in what percentage of incoming freshmen achieve B.A. degrees in six years. This measure of institutional success in freshmen actually finishing the degree has gained prominence in the last several years. When applying to a school, know the graduation rate of the prospective university. Avoid schools with low completion rates. No matter what such universities cost, they're not worth it.

A societal focus on the monetary value of a B.A. degree has changed how many young people look at the college experience. One researcher found that

70 percent of the students surveyed reported that social learning was more important than academics, referring to learning as "work" and social learning as "fun." Don't settle for fun. Start your career while you're in school by working at learning.

Choosing a university is an important step in pursuing education, but the rankings that get the most media attention are flawed. Theater program accreditation is generally of little significance in the choice. (Accreditation may be of some significance when evaluating non-degree-granting institutions since accreditation demonstrates a minimum level of educational professionalism.) No single factor can determine which theater program is best for which student.

Beyond the facts lie opinions. Here are some of ours. Choosing a university is stressful for many students and parents. There is no substitute for gathering facts and considering them in terms of the individual student. There is no way to get enough information to know for certain in advance if the choice will be right for the individual. It follows then that students should be prepared to transfer to a different school if the first choice isn't right. And transfer as soon as possible. No one should be a passive bystander concerning his or her education and career.

CHAPTER 4

Theater Career Income Varies

Making a successful, financially secure, and meaningful career is difficult, not just for people in theater but for everyone. Armed with facts when making career plans can improve the chance of success in any career endeavor. This chapter reports the facts on the earning power of theater workers with data from multiple sources, some national and some local, some statistically sound and some anecdotal. Whatever differences exist among the findings from these various sources, the inference remains clear: making a secure living in theater alone can be highly chancy. However, looking at drama careers in isolation doesn't tell a complete story. So we compare career results of people holding business undergraduate degrees with those who are drama graduates. On average business majors make more money than drama majors, but the range of salaries for both majors overlaps significantly.

There are many sources for facts about career prospects in theater. The sources cited in this chapter differ in approach, sampling, and definitions, so the data they supply can confuse a casual reader. Some of the facts reported here get close to basic information on theater careers but not always as close as we would prefer. For example, some surveys lump "theater" with more general topics like "performing arts." However, even allowing for these differences, the studies cited here essentially agree.

Several national surveys provide statistically sound reports. We report on five of them. The U.S. Census Bureau does many surveys in addition to its constitutionally required census each decade. Some surveys it conducts under its own budget, and others it performs under contracts funded by other entities. The National Science Foundation, unexpectedly, provides important data on theater practitioners. And nongovernment survey assessments also offer telling information.

Some may say, "Oh, that's just *one* survey." We have included multiple sources to offer a complete and fairly consistent picture of job chances for theater workers. Once all the facts are considered, it is impossible to deny that theater people, on average, have a difficult time making remunerative careers.

American Community Survey

This survey shows that theater and other media professionals historically earn less than the average worker. However, the number of media jobs is increasing at a little more than the average rate.

The U.S. Census Bureau augments its regular census with a yearly "American Community Survey" (ACS). This yearly survey, focused specifically on employment and earnings, defines its categories in ways that are not perfect for investigating theater employment. Note the relevant employee classifications and their definitions:

> Actors: *stage*, television, radio, video, or motion picture;
> Dancers and choreographers;
> Designers: commercial and industrial designers, fashion designers, floral designers, graphic designer, interior designers, merchandise displayers and window trimmers, *set* and exhibit designers;
> Producers and directors: *stage*, television, radio, video, or motion pictures;
> Writers and authors: scripts, stories, novels, poems, *plays*, biographies, advertisements, speeches, and other material. Does not include technical writers, editors, or journalists.

We have added the italics to highlight theater jobs included with others in the ACS definitions.

The figures the ACS collects, then, include people who work in theater with others who work similar jobs in different media. Still, the ACS reports how many jobs exist in artistic careers, including theater jobs, during each survey year. Comparing years reveals whether jobs in artistic careers are shrinking, growing, or unchanged.

The ACS classifies a respondent's job as being the one worked the most hours during the week before the survey. Thus there may be many people who consider themselves theater workers who, if they didn't have a theater job during the survey week, are not counted here. That means this survey is a profile of *working* actors, dancers, choreographers, and others *at one moment in time*.

The American Community Survey reveals that the number of artistic workers has been growing at a rate slightly higher than the growth of the total civilian work force in each theater-related classification except one. The number of producers and directors has increased at less than the rate of the population; in the five years between 2000 and 2005 it's grown only 0.5 percent. (See appendix A for a table based on the ACS that reveals specific increases in various theatre jobs.)

Because of its methodology, the ACS's total number of actors—stage, television, radio, video, and motion picture—was 41,742 in 2005, about as many actors as there are members of the stage actors union alone, Actors' Equity Association (Equity). This anomaly exists because a large percentage actors are not working as actors at any given time. The percentages of artistic workers in media that include theater who are employed full-year, full-time according to the ACS follow:

15.1 percent of actors
24.9 percent of dancers
61.5 percent of designers
65.6 percent of producers and directors
51.9 percent of writers

Many of these creative workers in all media are *self-employed*. For example, the ACS reports, 29.7 percent of actors are self-employed compared to just 10.2 percent of the civilian labor force. Median income is lower for actors and dancers than for the civilian labor force as a whole, even when comparing only those with full-year, full-time employment. For creative workers other than actors—dancers and choreographers, designers, producers and directors, and writers and authors—median income is higher than the labor force on average. (See appendix A for a table that shows the average income of all civilian workers compared to theater workers in specific areas.)

Five-Year Census Bureau Information

Census Bureau reports find that theater workers are less likely than the average worker to be employed full-time. They also earn less.

Every five years the census samples employers—entities with one or more paid employees, both full- and part-time—and extrapolates the data over the U.S. population. In its 2007 sample, the Census Bureau found 3,423 theaters and dinner theaters, employing a little more than 69,000 people. These sampled employers include commercial and not-for-profit (NFP) theaters. The total salary expenditures for theaters was estimated to be just under $2 billion. By dividing the salary expenditures by the number of employees, the average salary for a worker for a theater in the United States can be calculated. That *average salary* was $28,844 in 2007. The average salary for all businesses with employees in the United States, calculated in the same manner, was $41,310.

The average theater salary varied significantly by state. The lowest was Alaska at $11,186, the highest was Nevada at $59,011, and the average theater employee in New York State received $48,984 in salary. More than half of all employer theaters have between one and four employees. Most of them are very small entities.

In summary, the various Census Bureau reports show that

job growth in the artistic areas including theater is generally the same as the growth in the job market for the United States as a whole

artistic workers are less likely to be employed full-time
actors' salaries are lower than average salaries
average salaries for all theater employees are less than average salaries
for the U.S. work force as a whole

U.S. Bureau of Labor Statistics' Occupational Outlook

The government predicts job growth for most theater workers will be roughly average in the near term when compared to the growth in the entire job market. The U.S. Bureau of Labor Statistics publishes an annual survey called *Occupational Outlook*. The outlook combines statistics from a number of areas to project whether classes of jobs will increase or decline in a ten-year period. For 2008–18, the Bureau projects that job growth will be

average for actors, with 7,200 additional jobs for actors (13 percent growth)
average for directors and producers, with 9,700 additional jobs for directors
and producers (10 percent growth)
faster than average for makeup artists at 500 new jobs or 17 percent growth
slower than average for dancers and choreographers with 900 new jobs for
dancers (7 percent) and 900 new jobs for choreographers (5 percent).

The bureau projects the number of jobs for artistic workers then will grow at generally the same rate as the total job market, with exceptions for dancers and choreographers and makeup artists.

The Bureau of Labor Statistics acknowledges that its projections in the 2008–18 *Occupational Outlook* do not include adjustments for the impact of the recession that technically began in December 2007.

Visible Economy, LLC

Jobs for young people in the arts with university degrees, according to a special look at raw census data, have been increasing at an average rate in recent years. Visible Economy, LLC, provides information about *young* jobholders. It extracted government population study data to identify changes in numbers of employed university grads aged twenty-five to thirty-four in various job classes for the year ending August 2010. This age group might be considered a proxy for the people who are starting their careers, many by finding entry-level work. By tracking changes in numbers of young people employed in different jobs, the study identified where more jobs opened for young people and, conversely, where fewer jobs were available.

Visible Economy found the big growth areas for young university graduates in 2009–10 were in government, professional and technical services, hotels and restaurants, and social assistance. Jobs in the broad class of "arts, entertainment, and recreation" increased by 11,900 jobs that year for people twenty-four to thirty-four years old. The study revealed that there were more new jobs created in the arts than were created, for example, in Internet publishing and broadcasting (7,000) but fewer jobs than were created in health care (20,700).

Both the Bureau of Labor Statistics projections and the Visible Economy measurements are moderately reassuring facts for young people seeking a career in theater. The job market in theater is not shrinking. It is growing at an average rate.

National Science Foundation

Using raw data collected for the National Science Foundation, we find that drama B.A. holders earn less than average for all college grads. Drama graduates are more likely to be teachers. A comforting note—if *schadenfreude*—may be that English majors earn even less than drama majors. This survey looks at workers in all stages of life.

Based on the NSF survey (See appendix B for a more specific description of the survey), statistics prepared for this book show that holders of at least a B.A. in dramatic arts

earned less money than the average holder of at least a B.A., $46,415 compared to $68,455;

were, on average, the same age as the population as a whole, forty-seven years old, so neither age nor experience accounts for the difference in average salary;

were less likely to work full-time compared to the population average: 80.3 percent of drama majors worked full-time versus 89.8 percent for the general population.

The NSF figures also show that drama grads are

less likely to work at a for-profit business than the population average (35.9 percent versus 54.4 percent);

a little more likely to be self-employed or work for a not-for-profit organization;

more likely to teach in two- and four-year colleges than average (39.7 percent versus 23.8 percent);

a little less likely to work for federal or state government.

Dramatic arts majors who earn B.A. degrees are much more likely to be female than the general population. Women made up about 62.8 percent of drama grads versus 43.0 percent for the graduate population as a whole. Although recent years have seen improvement in the comparative earning power of women, they still make less, on average, than men. In 2003, the year of this survey, women in the general population earned about 75.5 percent of what men earned. However, gender differences can explain only a part of the reduced average wages for drama graduates.

Although historically more men than women received college degrees, this proportion has changed. About 57 percent of enrollees at U.S. colleges have been women since at least 2000, according to a recent report by the American Council on Education. The U.S. Bureau of the Census projects that the percentage of undergraduate and postgraduate enrollment that is female will continue to grow over the next decade. The census reported that as of 2010 roughly equal numbers of men and women who are twenty-five years of age or older hold undergraduate degrees, approximately 30 percent. This change is significant. In 1970, for example, the percentages were 7.8 for men and 5.8 for women.

Drama majors were

less likely to marry than average (48.8 percent versus 74.6 percent), whether for economic or personal reasons is unknown;
somewhat more likely to define their race as white than average (79.3 percent versus 71.8 percent).

The differences in race for dramatic arts B.A. degrees was almost totally because of the small percentage of Asians with dramatic arts degrees compared to the percentage of Asians in the university graduate population as a whole (1.6 percent drama graduates versus 11.7 percent of all graduates). The percentage of African Americans was virtually equal in dramatic arts majors and in the survey population as a whole, about 7 percent.

Compared to the general population of university graduates, drama BAs are

more likely to describe their work to be *unrelated to their highest degree* (29.4 percent contrasted to 15.3 percent);
about as likely as the average graduate to report that they are *satisfied* or *very satisfied* with their current work, at 89.5 percent compared to 90.6 percent.

As discussed in chapter 2, a liberal arts degree is a generalist degree, not a professional degree, so it is not surprising that a significant portion of B.A. holders work in areas unrelated to the subject matter of their undergraduate majors.

In an effort to understand the relative financial standing of dramatic arts majors with other typical majors, we searched the NSF data set for two other areas: English language and literature majors and business administration and general business majors. The most popular major with undergraduates in recent years has been a B.A. in business. (See Appendix B for a detailed chart of the data we found.) The comparison among these majors, taken as examples, show some expected differences and some that are surprising:

Business majors on average earn more than dramatic arts majors; English majors earn less.

Business majors were much less likely to be female than the other two
degree majors.

Business majors are more likely to say that their current job is only somewhat related to their degree specialty than either English or dramatic arts
majors would.

A small percentage (about 2 percent) of all groups reported they are very
dissatisfied with their current jobs.

Given the large number of employer classifications used in the NSF survey,
it is difficult to give a quick, general view of the industries in which the holders
of dramatic arts B.A. degrees currently work. Very generally, then, the biggest
employers of dramatic arts graduates are motion picture and video and, by far,
teaching. There is some clustering in the professional and consulting areas and in
banking and allied professions. As noted earlier, a significant number of dramatic
arts graduates are self-employed.

Playwrights

Playwrights are a special case of theater workers, for they are rarely employees of
producers or NFP theaters and thus are not usually represented in many surveys
of salaried theater workers. Rather, playwrights work mostly "on spec," a short
way of saying that playwrights write *speculatively*, without a contract or option,
in hopes that a script will attract a commercial producer or not-for-profit artistic
director to stage it. Sometimes an established playwright will receive a commission to write a play for a theater for some special occasion or to write the book
for a musical, but that is less common.

A playwright has several sources of potential income from a play: option
money, royalties, and subsidiary rights. The most significant money for a successful play is the royalty payment from weekly gross ticket sales, in the commercial theater typically 5 percent until the investment is recouped and 10 percent
thereafter.

When a producer or not-for-profit theater wants to produce a script, it
obtains an option. The playwright receives a payment in return for an exclusive
commitment that the option buyer may stage the work if the production opens
in some limited time period, typically six months. The option will specify that
the option can be renewed for additional periods in exchange for more option
payments. If no production is staged during this time, all rights revert to the
playwright, who keeps the options payments and can seek options from others.
This option is different than the license that a local theater or school obtains to
stage an existing script. For one thing, the option agreement gives the producer
or not-for-profit theater certain long-term rights if the original production is
successful. The theory supporting this sharing of the playwright's earnings is that
the producer or not-for-profit theater, by taking the significant monetary risks of

mounting a successful production of the play, increases the value of the play and so deserves a share of the subsidiary profits.

For a commercial production, subsidiary rights include a share of the author's payments from

film, television, and other stage productions;
productions in other media, perhaps as much as 50 percent of the playwright's earnings;
stock theater productions, typically 50 percent for five years and 25 percent for the next three years after that;
revivals staged in the next 40 years, typically 20 percent;
commercial merchandise, such as dolls, clothing, and so on.

Commercial theater producer Jim Freydberg has said, "Broadway isn't where you make the money any more. It's where you establish the project so you can make the money. When you mount a show now, you really have to think about where it's going to play later." Freydberg's may be an extreme point of view, but it emphasizes the importance of subsidiary rights to the value of an option.

Not-for-profit theaters producing premieres also require playwrights to share their subsequent earnings from the script, typically 10 percent or less of playwright royalties. This share of royalties is in addition to the not-for-profit theater sharing in the commercial producers' profits from a subsequent commercial run.

However, sometimes even Broadway flops can provide playwrights a nice income from subsidiary rights. Consider *All Shook Up,* the Elvis Presley musical, which grossed just more than $12 million in thirty-two weeks on Broadway in 2005, rarely running at 75 percent or more of theater capacity. A *New York Times* review declared, "Yet another synthetic jukebox musical opened last night on Broadway, fresh off the assembly line." In its annual tote of Broadways "hits and misses," *Variety* called *All Shook Up* a miss, meaning it did not return its investors' money. Joe DePietro, the book author of *All Shook Up,* said, "I made tens of thousands of dollars from my first quarterly royalty check for the stock and amateur rights. I could barely make a living with *All Shook Up* on Broadway. I bought a nice country house [from] *All Shook Up* in stock and amateur [royalties]."

Of the 2006 flop *The Wedding Singer,* the composer Matthew Sklar said, "It hasn't made me a rich person, but it has allowed me to write two more shows in the last two years. There are usually 60–70 productions of *Wedding Singer* being planned at a time." The off-Broadway *succès d'estime* musical *The Last Five Years* is the financial "bedrock" of composer Jason Robert Brown's career. "If the only validation I got in this business was from the reception of my shows in New York City, I'd be doing something else by now," he said.

These unusual examples aside, playwrights as a group are not making substantial incomes from playwriting; most of their earnings come from activities unrelated to playwriting, according to a survey by the Theatre Development Fund.

> The average playwright responding to the survey earned between $25,000 and $39,000 per year from all sources. Almost two-thirds of playwrights made less than $40,000 yearly. Twenty-two percent made $60,000 or more and only 9.5 percent made more than $100,000 yearly.
> Only 15 percent of earnings, on average, came from theatrical productions of plays. About 15 percent came from writing for television or film.
> A little more than one-fifth of the income on average came from teaching.
> Just more than 50 percent of playwrights' income came from sources totally unrelated to playwriting.

As the study's authors lamented, "The economics of playwriting are akin to those of a hobby; you might make a bit of cash by buying and selling old comic books, but you don't plan to live off it." In an interview in 2011, Tony Kushner, author of the Tony Award and Pulitzer Prize winning *Angels in America*, said, "I make my living now as a screenwriter! Which I'm surprised and horrified to find myself saying, but I don't think I can support myself as a playwright at this point. I don't think anybody does."

Most important, the Theatre Development Fund survey sought out working professional playwrights, people who have had productions on major stages, sometimes received prestigious awards, and often completed an M.F.A. in playwriting and/or attended important playwriting conferences. If wannabe playwrights were also surveyed, the dollar figures for average playwright earnings would be grimmer.

Jobs in NFP Theaters

There is a source for a comfortable living in theater—probably even health benefits—by working for a successful, *large*, not-for-profit professional theater, especially in management or administration. To a limited extent information about these jobs can be found in IRS records. Not-for-profit groups' IRS reports, Form 990, are public records and are available on a number of websites with searching capabilities, such as the Foundation Center, http://foundationcenter .org/findfunders/990finder/.

Not-for-profit organizations file tax returns, IRS Form 990, even though they are not federally taxed. Unlike an individual's tax return, the 990 filings are public records. The intent, at least in part, is to provide the community the not-for-profit serves the same kind of basic financial data that a stockholder in a publicly traded corporation would have through Security Exchange Commission filings and annual reports, so the community can decide whether to continue to support the not-for-profit corporation. In addition to sources of revenue, expenditures, and the like, the 990s report any money paid to board members and salary and wages for the top five employees. Thus the 990s give some information on salaries in the not-for-profit theater.

The stunning fact is that few small theaters, that is, those with budgets of less than $1 million, pay anyone but the artistic or executive director who typically founded the NFP theater. In 2011 Rocco Landesman, chairman of the National Endowment for the Arts and co-owner of the Jujamcyn Broadway theaters, asked a provocative question: "There are 5.7 million arts workers in this country and two million artists. Do we need three administrators for every artist?" The economic differences between arts administrators and artists include profound differences between theater administrators and theater artists, as our findings from IRS records for NFP theaters show.

Because NFP theaters of different budget sizes have different patterns of staffing, we have separated this discussion into three parts: small-, medium-, and large-budget theaters.

Small NFP Theaters

Non-Equity theaters do not generally publish their payments to actors. Small theaters—those with budgets less than one-half million dollars—often pay no salaries. As budgets grow, the first salaried staff are typically an artistic director and an executive director. The next employee may be a secretary. As budget sizes grow, the typical staff added to the payroll are development directors, marketing directors, and financial staff, such as controllers. If the theater presents new plays, a literary manager may be the next hire when the budget grows to support another addition to payroll.

Some examples can make the amounts of compensation more vivid. Founded in 1996, Brat Productions in Philadelphia produces contemporary material and reenvisioned classics, working in nontraditional venues and with low ticket prices. Its budget in 2009 was $122,650. Of that, the producing artistic director received a salary of $28,376. Total salaries were $37,729, and professional fees were $25,925.

Centre Stage in Greenville, South Carolina, has a budget a little in excess of one-half million and in its 2008 IRS filing reported paying its executive director $36,000 yearly, although in that year, the director loaned the salary back to the company to solve cash-flow problems! Founded in 1983, Centre Stage is a year-round, 285-seat regional theater, offering revivals of musicals and comedies and a new play festival. When Centre Stage hires Equity actors, it uses the guest artist contract. Under a guest artist contract, no more than two union actors may be employed in any one production. No Equity actor is required to be cast on any production according to the contract. Minimum union salaries range from $300 to $510 weekly depending on number of performances per week, plus a $22 per diem and housing that consists of at least a bedroom. For non-Equity actors no information is available.

Medium NFP Theaters

A 2010 article in the *Theatre Bay Area* magazine profiled a few medium-sized theaters in the San Francisco area. The Cutting Ball Theatre has a budget of about $350,000 and employs three full-time staff to produce three shows a year seen by audiences numbering about 5,000 total. Its nonunion actors are paid a stipend of $1,000 *per production*. The Cutting Ball artistic director received a salary of $33,417 according to the 2009 IRS filing. Shotgun Players is significantly larger, offering six productions a year with a budget of about $700,000. It hires Equity actors under the guest artist contract and pays nonunion actors a stipend of $1,500 to $2,000 *per production*. An estimate of a living wage for a one-person household in San Francisco, a notoriously expensive place to live, is $506 weekly or $26,312 yearly.

Budget size and location do not in themselves define actor fees. In the Bay Area, the Jewish Theatre and City Lights have about the same budget of $600,000 yearly and the same number of full-time staff, four. Because the Jewish Theatre rent is unusually low, it can afford to pay actors under the Equity Bay Area Theatre, Tier 3, agreement of $413 per week. City Lights offers its nonunion actors $150 per production. City Lights paid its executive artistic director a salary of $29,300 as of its 2006 IRS report and its associate artistic director/production manager $39,101. The Jewish Theatre paid its executive director and artistic director $52,000 each, according to its 2007 IRS filing.

Large NFP Theaters

The picture is more pleasing at theaters with larger budgets. Geffen Playhouse in Los Angeles has a budget of just a little more than $9 million. Founded in 1995, it focuses on new play development. The artistic director's salary is more than $140,000, and the executive director's salary is more than $123,000. Geffen Playhouse has a development director who is paid $122,838 yearly and a half-time stage director who is paid $38,077. Geffen is a LORT-B theater, and, as such, Equity minimums are $750 per week. LORT-B theaters may hire actors who are not members of Equity under certain conditions, the salary to be negotiated between the theater and the actor. (For a description of LORT theaters and their classifications by budget, see the sidebar on page 21.)

The Lincoln Center Theatre is generally regarded as the richest not-for-profit theater in the United States, with a budget of more than $66 million in 2009. This total budget was a great increase from the previous year's budget of $34 million, probably a result of the success, increased revenue, and increased costs of the revival of the musical *South Pacific*. In 2009 Lincoln Center Theatre's income from ticket sales also saw a great increase, to $54 million from $18 million. Its artistic director and executive director are each paid close to one-half million dollars a year. Its development director is paid $260,000, production manager $200,000, casting director $172,000, and wardrobe supervisor $173,000. Three of Lincoln Center Theatre's stage technicians earn about $200,000 a year. Minimum actor salaries are $1,207 weekly, and if the production is extended beyond its originally scheduled run, the minimum goes up to $1,653.

One of the actors in *South Pacific* is listed with the top-paid individuals in the organization during the reporting year of 2009. Loretta Ables Sayre, a well-respected actor from Hawaii, played Bloody Mary in the Rodgers and Hammerstein musical and received $299,000 yearly.

Because many larger not-for-profit theaters are year-round operations, staff positions can pay a livable salary, and many offer benefits such as health insurance for full-time employees. Actors, however, are sometimes paid less than a living wage at smaller regional theaters.

Teaching Public School

In the mid–twentieth century, it was somewhat commonplace for parents to say to their—usually female—child, "Well, become a schoolteacher. You'll never be rich, but you can get a job wherever you go." This cliché has become less true over time, at both ends of the spectrum. Public school teachers still won't become rich on their salaries, but the public and political attention given in the last few decades to academic standards and unified testing in public education have gradually increased salaries for public school teachers. According to the Bureau of Labor Statistics in 2009, secondary education drama teacher jobs earned an average salary of $54,620. Teachers receive health benefits and pension plans. Like some public school athletic personnel, a few drama teachers/directors at high schools with celebrated theater programs get more money than at others.

Yet in the quest to do better on standardized testing and working under budget pressures, many school districts have reduced or eliminated arts programs in their schools, including drama programs. In a 2002 survey, only 19 percent of elementary schools had programs in drama, and only 48 percent of secondary schools offered drama education. "Secondary schools" means middle, junior, and high schools. For secondary schools *with drama programs*, 89 percent had at least one full-time teacher in drama, and the rest had part-time teachers. About one-quarter of secondary schools received at least some support for their drama programs from sources other than the school budget. A 2004 survey of school principals found that 25 percent of schools had cut instructional time for the arts, and 33 percent expected additional cuts in the future.

If one is searching for artistic expression in a theater career, public school teaching may be frustrating in the twenty-first century. Theater art in the public schools is made through the students with whatever capabilities and interests they have. In addition to the workday, drama teachers in secondary schools are generally required to produce one, two, or more stage productions each year, rehearsing with students after the school day and on weekends. At least public school teachers have the vaunted summer months free and could seek freelance theater work during those months.

In summary public school teaching salaries have risen in recent years. Yet arts programs have been the among the early casualties of budget pressures in an era of standardized testing. There is no standardized testing for drama used to evaluate student progress. Since drama and the other arts are not included in standardized testing, drama and the other arts are easier to cut from budgets in bad economic times. Many experts are concerned because they project that arts programs in the public schools will continue to shrink. In addition the work of teaching theater in the public schools is more about having a positive impact on the growth of young people than it is about the teachers' personal artistic fulfillment.

College and University Teaching

Teaching theater in a college or university *can* offer artistic expression. To receive tenure for professors who are eligible for tenure—those hired in so-called tenure-track positions—one is generally expected to produce, in time-honored phrasing, either "scholarship that adds to the body of knowledge in one's field" or "artistic expression equivalent to scholarship." For the purposes of receiving tenure, "artistic expression" often does not include productions created at one's own university, so getting hired elsewhere for artistic work is important to job retention and promotion.

Life tenure is a senior academic's contractual right not to have his or her position terminated without just cause. With some exceptions, a new university teacher in a tenure-track position will be at the assistant professor level. (People with outstanding records of achievement in the field may be hired *with* tenure. Professors currently holding tenure somewhere may decide that they will only transfer to a job at a new school if that job comes with tenure.) After some years of employment, the assistant professor will be assessed by several layers of academic committees and individuals, reviewing the quantity and quality of teaching, service to the university and profession, and scholarship or artistic achievement. If the teacher does not meet standards, there may be more time to improve performance. But there is usually a limited period one can stay at the assistant professor level, typically seven years. The job is "up-or-out": *up* to associate or full professor and tenure or *out* to some other job. Once tenure is received, most universities allot "release time," a less-than-normal teaching load, so the professor can pursue scholarship or artistic achievement. In addition most schools offer tenured professors a sabbatical, a one-semester or one-year paid release from service every seven years, to pursue scholarship or artistic achievement.

Senior faculty typically get to teach the best students and so are involved in students' artistic expression and growth. Many professors actively create theater in their own schools: designing sets, costumes, or lighting; directing students and maybe guest professional actors; or acting lead roles.

Not all openings at the university level are tenure-track positions. Most U.S. universities also use nontenured adjunct professors, academics who teach classes for lower wages and fewer employment benefits under short-term contracts. Some may demonstrate such competence that the school will consider them for hiring should a tenure-track position open, but no such promotion is implied in being hired for an adjunct position. Additionally schools with graduate programs use their graduate students to teach courses as part of the requirements of work-study financial aid.

As a result of using the less expensive adjunct professors and graduate students in the classroom, since 1972 the percentage of college and university teaching positions in the United States that are either tenured or tenure-track has steadily declined. The U.S. Department of Education put the combined tenured/tenure-track rate at 56 percent for 1975, 46.8 percent for 1989, and 31.9 percent for 2005. By 2005, 48 percent of teachers in U.S. universities were part-time employees. The American Association of University Professors reported in 2003 that the "proportion of faculty who are appointed each year to tenure-line positions is declining at an alarming rate."

Salaries for university professors can be attractive. In 2009–10, the average salary for *all* full professors in the United States at schools awarding doctorates was $125,300, while it was $83,511 for all associate professors and $71,485 for all assistant professors. Non-tenure-track positions were paid significantly less. Instructors' average salary was $48,138, and lecturers' was $54,583. (The difference between the duties of an instructor and a lecturer may be hard to discern at many schools.) The salary rates are lower at schools offering only the baccalaureate degree. Average professors' salary in such universities was $87,013, average associates' was $67,077, average assistants' was $55,495.

A 2008 survey by the College and University Association for Human Resources revealed that the three disciplines with the lowest full-professor average salaries were English; visual and performing arts; and parks, recreation, leisure, and fitness studies.

Being a professor of theater in a university or college can be a good gig, with a living wage and benefits and artistic challenges and fulfillment possible. But the "up-or-out" structure of professorship at most schools puts pressure on achievement within the terms of a given school's tenure and promotion standards and practices. Moreover many schools are filling fewer tenure-track positions, and some schools are awarding tenure for a smaller number of tenure-track professors. Administrations find that it is cheaper and offers more flexibility to employ part-time adjunct instructors and lecturers or graduate students.

The Trouble with Comparing Averages

The troubles with considering average salaries across different fields or undergraduate degrees are many. First, no one sets out to be average. Each young person is encouraged to believe he or she has the stuff to be above average. And often one-half of all people in any given measure are above average. Few people think about the opposite fact: one-half are usually *below* average. To oversimplify the mathematics of statistics, when the measurements in a sample or a population are evenly distributed, there will be the same number of instances above and below the median, and the median will be virtually identical to the average. There are populations or samples that are not evenly distributed, hence the use of the adverb *often*.

More important, average results don't reveal the often significant amounts of variation in a measure. Earlier in this chapter, some average salaries were reported for B.A. degrees in dramatic arts and in business, based on data collected for the National Survey of College Graduates. Business majors on average made a higher salary than dramatic arts majors, $62,853 versus $46,415. No matter how big the difference in average salaries, however, one cannot infer that every business graduate makes more than every drama graduate. Consider fig. 4. More dramatic arts graduates make less than $60,001 per year than do business grads, and the opposite is true, as well: more business graduates make $60,001 or more per year than do dramatic arts graduates. However, the two distributions of salaries overlap significantly. There are dramatic arts graduates who make more than $120,000 per year, and there are business degree holders making $15,000 or less. Whatever the averages say, the outcome for an individual is just that: *individual*. However, dramatic arts majors should know they start out with a disadvantage to some of their peers with other subject majors.

Beyond the Facts

Ignore economic data presented in this chapter at your peril. Those interested in making theater a career will find the statistics are consistent, compelling, and discouraging. Theater professionals make less money than average and typically do not work in their art full-time. The clear inference is that young people looking for a career in theater would be wise to develop skills to support themselves between theater jobs.

That said, there is no undergraduate degree that is a slam dunk to a financially rewarding career. Holders of bachelor degrees in business administration, for example, on average do financially better than those with dramatic arts majors,

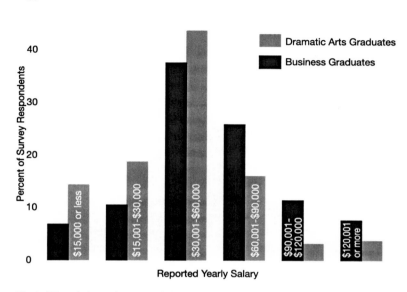

Fig. 4. Although dramatic arts graduates on average make less than business graduates, there is total overlap of the distribution of salaries for the two majors. If one knows two people, one a dramatic arts graduate and one a business graduate, one cannot say which person has a higher salary based on their undergraduate majors alone. Source: National Survey of College Graduates, October 2003.

but at every salary level the earnings for the two degrees overlap. Both degree holders when surveyed in national polls express nearly identical levels of satisfaction with their current work.

Theater people are not the only ones who find it hard to make a living. In January 2011 the *New York Times* reported that many graduates of law schools have a hard time finding jobs in their fields. Even when they have passed the bar exam and are licensed to practice, many struggle. There is nothing that is a sure thing for any career path.

Beyond the facts lie opinion. Here are some of ours. There are disciplines other than live theater where many theatrical skills are appropriate. These jobs are not included in *Theater Careers.* They include the obvious candidates:

Film and television clearly have positions parallel to those of live theater— actors, directors, designers, and administrative positions.

Modeling jobs require many skills that actors develop.

Commercials use all acting "types," from the young to the old and the trim
to the overweight, and the pay can be quite satisfying. Many stage actors
work in commercials.

Trade shows or industrials employ many of the positions outlined in this
chapter.

In reviewing anecdotal information about these theater-related fields, we
found a range of earnings and an uneven pattern of employment that are similar
to the patterns of earnings and employment in the legitimate theater itself. A
recent issue of *Entertainment Weekly* estimates that 80 percent of Screen Actors
Guild members are unemployed. The Screen Actors Guild is the union of film
and television actors. The Writers Guild of America West, the union of film and
television writers, reports that a little more than one-half of its members are
employed in any year.

Sound and lighting designers sometimes have businesses renting equipment
to hotels, convention centers, and the like. These nontheater jobs can make money
and also keep the designers in touch with people in their community who might
use their design skills. Designers, especially lighting designers, can find work even
further afield, designing lighting for restaurants, corporate meeting spaces, product introductions, conventions, religious sanctuaries and meeting halls, political
conventions, and the like.

CHAPTER 5

Theatrical Unions Make Rules but Not Jobs

Unions are organizations of workers, united to negotiate with employers. When first formed in the United States, the unions were an important redress to often egregious domination of employees by their employers. Union membership in the United States as a whole has waxed and waned over time, but it's been steadily declining since 1983. Currently about 12 percent of the civilian workforce is represented by unions.

Today, as throughout their history, unions are controversial. Federal labor laws now reduce the worst maltreatment of employees, prompting some to argue that unions are unnecessary and that they inflate labor costs in ways that hurt the international competitiveness of U.S. industry. Labor unions typically operate political arms that largely support Democratic candidates probably because the Democratic Party historically has been more supportive of unions than the Republican Party. This political action breeds resentment from those not receiving union support.

The Nature of Labor Unions

In some states, so-called *union shops* or *agency shops* are legal. In those shops all new employees must join a union after a minimum period or must pay dues even if they don't join the union. On the other hand, *right-to-work* laws exist in twenty-two states, mostly in the South and West, which prohibit employers from making membership or payment of union dues a condition of employment.

Theater Unions

The earliest theater employees to organize were the stagehands. Their union, the National Alliance of Theatrical Stage Employees (now the International Alliance of Theatrical Stage Employees or IATSE) was founded in 1910. The Dramatists Guild was formed in 1912.* The Actors' Equity Association (Equity) began in 1913.

---

* The Dramatists Guild is no longer a union because of court rulings that playwrights and composers are not employees of producers or NFP theaters under law. The guild still exists as a trade association.

As an example of the conditions early unions were battling, consider what led to the founding of Equity. In the late nineteenth and early twentieth centuries, theater work was dominated by the Theatre Syndicate. Essentially a monopoly, the syndicate could blackball any performer who opposed it or disagreed with its procedures. Even acclaimed actors of the early twentieth century, such as Sarah Bernhardt and Minnie Maddern Fiske, were reduced to playing in run-down auditoriums and tents when they opposed the syndicate. The working conditions for actors before the union was founded were distressing. Rehearsals were unpaid and of any length; actors were paid solely for performances. Actors had to supply their own costumes. Backstage was often dirty, unheated, or sweltering, with no running water and thus no toilets. Productions could close suddenly, leaving the performers without pay or, if on the road, without transportation home.

Over time, Equity has

required producers to buy bonds which guaranteed that salaries earned
would be paid should a production suddenly fold;
negotiated minimum salaries and rehearsal pay;
regulated safe and sanitary workplaces;
enforced restrictions on the employment of foreign actors;
established protections for actors and stage managers in dealings with
theatrical agents and producers.

Today it offers pension and health-care benefits for some members and promotes safety rules to protect actors on increasingly dangerous computer-controlled stages. Other theatrical workers' unions attempt similar aims: negotiating and policing employers, establishing minimum wages and work conditions, and offering health and pension plans.

Broadway unions remain strong even as unions in many industries have been losing ground. Labor disputes in the entertainment industry have a public impact that is out of proportion to the number of jobs involved. Stage artists know how to work publicity channels. Image is important to theater producers so they try to avoid labor actions. Producers cannot hire replacement workers to continue work during a strike for several reasons. Audiences in the theater district won't, for the most part, cross picket lines. A star, an actor whose name is above the title and whose appearance is one reason tickets are sold, is irreplaceable by a nonunion performer. When Broadway musicians struck in 2003, producers considered using synthesizers to replace the striking musicians. However, other theater unions vowed not to cross the musician union's picket lines so all musicals except one stopped performing for four days. (The show that was not affected by the strike had already concluded a contract with the musician's union.) It is unknown if audiences would have accepted the electronic substitutes for live musicians.

Should Someone Starting Out Join a Theatrical Union?

Outside of Broadway the extent of union membership and the importance of union membership for theatrical work varies widely. Joining a union won't get anyone a job. As already reported, union actors, directors, and designers have difficulty finding full-time work or its financial equivalent. Of course, nonunion theater workers also find it hard to support themselves. However, in some communities there will be more nonunion than union jobs. Although the pay will likely be less for nonunion than for union jobs, with little opportunity for health insurance or pensions, there can be more nonunion job openings. Union membership might *restrict* job availability, for example, in nonunion touring productions. Some shows—especially the third or fourth national tour of a musical, a tour that is playing short runs at smaller cities around the United States—are only profitable with lower-cost nonunion staffing.

Some theater teachers and casting directors advise that it is unwise to join a union too early and by doing so eliminate chances for valuable experience. Moreover, without experience, one may not be allowed to join some theatrical unions.

The unions vary in their willingness to publish information to outsiders about how membership is attained, what benefits accrue to members, and how much dues and fees cost. As with other facts about unions and union membership rules, the actor and stage manager union is the most forthcoming.

Actors' Equity Association

Equity represents actors and stage managers. Equity has a variety of contracts negotiated with different specific producers and NFP theaters or with groups of theaters and producers. Some contracts require that only Equity actors be hired, some require a certain number of Equity actors to be hired per production, and others allow a limited number of Equity actors to be hired but do not require any union actors to work on a given production. The following information about Equity was in effect as of January 2011.

Membership Requirements

If an actor or stage manager is hired by a producer or NFP theater with an Equity agreement, that person can and must join Equity during the term of the contract. Being hired for a union position when not a member already is not easy, however, as most commercial producers and some artistic directors will audition or interview only union members.

Actor unions in other media offer reciprocal membership. Members of the "Four A's,"—the Associated Actors and Artistes of America—including the Screen Actors Guild, American Federation of Television and Radio Artists, American Guild of Musical Artists, American Guild of Variety Artists, and the Guild of

Italian American Actors (SAG, AFTRA, AGMA, AGVA, or GIA) have agreed that the members of each union are professional actors and so may join any of the other unions with no other requirements except paying initiation fees and dues.

Alternatively there is the Equity Membership Candidate Program (EMC). This program permits actors and stage managers-in-training to credit nonunion work in an Equity theater toward membership in Equity. Eligibility under this program requires a total of fifty weeks of EMC work.

Fees and Dues

All membership privileges commence, including the right to vote at union meetings and attend Equity-only auditions, with the initial payment of $400 towards the initiation fee of $1100. The initiation fee is payable over a two-year period. Equity dues have two components: basic dues of $118 per year and working dues of 2.25 percent of gross earnings collected via weekly payroll deductions. Working dues apply to the first $300,000 per year of earnings.

Benefits

Equity members qualify for the pension fund by having five or ten years of vesting service, one year of vesting service is earned for each calendar year there are at least two weeks of Equity employment. Equity members qualify for health insurance by working at least twelve weeks of covered employment in the previous twelve months to qualify for six months of coverage. Twenty or more weeks of covered employment qualifies the member for twelve months of coverage. Both pension and health insurance are paid for by an assessment on Equity employers that is in addition to the minimum contract salary.

Rules of Membership

Equity requires that its members follow "rules of conduct which all members are expected to observe as professionals, for the dignity of the acting profession and the welfare of all their fellow performers" which include

> No rehearsal or performance without a signed contract;
> Giving the best possible performance as directed or choreographed; making no unauthorized changes in costume, make-up or hairstyle; taking proper care of all costumes; and appearing at curtain calls;
> On-time attendance for rehearsals and performances;
> No work with or without pay for any employer who is not a signatory to an Equity Agreement without prior written permission.

Earnings of Union and Some Nonunion Actors

There is much available data for the employment of union stage actors because Equity publishes detailed annual reports. The figures are grim:

Only 49.3 percent of Equity members worked in theater *at all* during
the 2008–9 season.

Average weeks worked in theater were 15.2.

Median earnings from theater work, for those members of Equity who
worked in the season at all, were $7,688.

Unlike in the findings of the National Survey of College Graduates, which surveyed holders of drama B.A. degrees and found they were more likely to be female
than male, actors who are members of the stage union are slightly more likely to
be male than female, 52.4 percent men versus 47.6 percent women.

The median salary hides a great deal of variance, revealed in fig. 5. More
members earned five thousand dollars or less than earned more than five thousand dollars.

Earnings of Equity Stage Actors
Yearly Earnings as Actors and Stage Managers by Numbers of Members

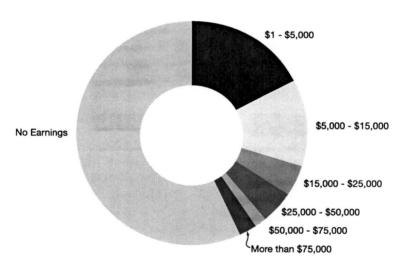

Fig. 5. Earnings of union stage actors vary, but most members make no money as
actors or stage managers in a given year. This chart is based on the 2006–7 Equity report
because Equity chose not to include this breakdown in the most recent annual report.
There is no reason to believe that the distribution has greatly changed.
Source: Actors Equity Association, "2006–2007 Theatrical Season Report."

Of course, stars can make much more. Daniel Craig and Hugh Jackman, starring
in 2009 in the Broadway drama *A Steady Rain,* earned nearly $100,000 each a
week, according to the *New York Post.* Although their base salary under contract
was only $40,000 a week, they got a percentage of the box office gross receipts.
The play ran for twelve weeks, with each actor paid about $1 million by the close

of the run. Most weeks this two-person drama grossed more than $1 million at the box office. Julia Roberts was said to earn more than $150,000 a week in the revival of *Three Days of Rain* on Broadway in 2006. Matthew Broderick and Nathan Lane each made more than $110,000 a week in *The Producers* and *The Odd Couple.* Stars are often worth the high pay. When David Hyde Pierce left the musical *Curtains* for vacation in 2007, box office fell by $240,000 a week according to *Variety.* When Catherine Zeta-Jones went on vacation from the revival of the Sondheim and Wheeler musical *A Little Night Music* in May 2010, box office grosses dropped from $917,526 to $485,701, a drop of more than $430,000. And when Nathan Lane took a vacation from the musical *The Addams Family* in August 2010, the show grossed $764,231, but the week before that, with Lane on stage, it had grossed $1,125,749. During Lane's break from the show, then, revenues dropped about one-third.

Chicago Actors

Outside of Broadway, figures for union and nonunion actors are sometimes available. In 2007 the *Chicago Tribune* reported the earnings prospects of Chicagoland actors. Three large Chicago theaters, the Goodman, the Court, and the Northlight, are members of the League of Resident Theatres (LORT). LORT members have Equity contracts that require standard union minimum pay for LORT theaters, ranging in 2008 from $544 to $840 per week minimum plus benefits, depending on the theater size. Even at LORT theaters not many actors work full-year, full-time.

Members of the Producers of Chicago Area Theatres (PCAT) have a separately negotiated contract with Equity. That contract covers about fifty producers and allows the producers to hire Equity and non-Equity actors under certain rules and proportions. PCAT union salary minimums in 2008 ranged from $162.50 to $700 weekly, depending on the potential box office gross of the venue.

Nonunion actors make less at the PCAT theaters. They also make less at Chicago-area theaters without Equity agreements. Some nonunion companies offer actors a *one-time* stipend ranging from $25 to $500, according to the *Chicago Tribune* report. Others offer *no money* or up to $200 per week. An estimate of a living wage for a one-person household in Chicago is $375 per week.

Colorado Actors

The *Denver Post* in 2006 reported the dilemma of union membership for Colorado actors: Equity membership offered more pay and the chance of working enough weeks to qualify for health insurance, but of Colorado's ninety-four theater companies only eight were Equity theaters in 2006. The dilemma for Colorado actors is that Equity membership might get an actor more money per week worked but there were fewer opportunities for an Equity actor to find work in

Colorado. Of Colorado theaters only the Denver Center Theatre Company is a member of LORT. Its minimum salary was $725 a week. For contrast, another Colorado Equity theater, the Aurora Fox, which is not a LORT theater, must hire at least two Equity actors per show. The Fox pays an Equity actor $177 per week plus pension and health benefits payments to the union and a non-Equity actor $150 per week—not much more than lunch money and carfare. An estimate of a living wage in Denver for a one-person household is $346 weekly.

The Stage Directors and Choreographers Society

Stage Directors and Choreographers Society (SDC) represents professional stage directors and choreographers throughout the United States. The SDC mission is "to foster a national community of professional Stage Directors and Choreographers by protecting the rights, health and livelihoods of all our Members. To facilitate the exchange of ideas, information and opportunities, while educating the current and future generations about the role of Directors and Choreographers and providing effective administration, negotiations and contractual support."

Membership

SDC membership requires proof of professional credits, which SDC defines as jobs on productions with union affiliations.

Associate membership is available to early-career directors and/or choreographers, college and university professionals, and community theater artists. The difference from full members is that associates may not file SDC contracts and do not qualify for pension and health benefits. The initiation fee and yearly dues for associates are significantly less than that of members.

Fees and Dues

Full members pay an initiation fee and yearly dues, plus an assessment on all fees and royalties earned under SDC contracts. Yearly dues are $150 for members; $50 for associates. Working dues are 2.5 percent of gross wages. The initiation fee is $1,000 for full members and $250 for associates.

Benefits

Members are eligible to participate in the health plan if they are employed under an SDC contract and sufficient employer contributions are made to the SDC-League Health Fund on their behalf. To be eligible for health benefits, employer contributions of at least $1,100 must be made in a six-month span. A member is eligible for a pension once they reach age sixty-five, provided that they are "vested," that is, that they have worked under SDC contracts subject to employer pension contributions in each of five years with no substantial break in service.

Some Earnings of Union and Nonunion Directors,
Choreographers, and Designers

The other creative unions for theater artists do not report how much their membership works or how much the members earn. Still there is relevant information. For example, table 3, below, shows some of the negotiated minimums for union directors, choreographers, and designers working in a range of producing situations. These are minimums, however, and in-demand artists can negotiate higher fees. The top fees are for Broadway, and they include royalty payments during the show run.

Table 3: Some Union Minimums

		Broadway		Off-Broadway		LORT A	LORT C
	Fee	Wkly Min	Royalty	Fee	Royalty	Fee	Fee
Director	$30,105	$650* or $1,300**	1.5%* or 3.5%**	$9,682	2%*	$25,000	$7,850
Choreographer	$20,630	$490* or $650**	0.5%* or 1%**	$7,746	1.5%*	$18,750	$5,888
Scenic Des.	$8,498	$305	$7,744				
Lighting Des.	$6,371	$305	0.425%**	not available		$5,776	$2,458
Costume Des.	$6,212	$305	0.425%**			$5,776	$2,458
Design Asst.	$1,382 weekly salary						

* Percent of (or minimum against the percent of) GWBOR: gross weekly box office receipts.

** Percent of WNOP: weekly net operating profit (GWBOR minus weekly expenses).

Notes: For this table, the minimum union fees were chosen for some representative engagements. There are many contracts, each with its own specifications and wage rates.

Producers or not-for-profit theaters make additional payments to those listed here, such as pension fund and health insurance assessments, lodging, and per diem. For Broadway directors, this table uses rates for drama. Musical rates are higher. The royalties are chosen by the director and choreographer when negotiating a contract with the producer. The rates for GWBOR rise for any week that box office significantly exceeds operating expenses. For Broadway designers this table uses rates for a drama with a single set and 1–7 characters. Other rates are higher. For off-Broadway, this chart uses rates for commercial runs in houses between 400–499 seats. Other rates are lower.

With the exception for union fees for touring productions and Las Vegas, minimum fees for union artists in other theaters are mostly lower than those in table 3. Nonunion theater artists generally receive even lower salaries and fees.

By contrast Broadway work can be very remunerative. Consider one director and one Broadway musical: Hal Prince and *The Phantom of the Opera.* From its Broadway opening in 1988 through June 27, 2011, *Phantom* grossed $816,647,772. *Phantom* was still running in New York at that time, filling 90 percent of seats. If Prince's contract called for the *minimum* royalty against gross box office receipts for a Broadway musical, 0.75%, he will have been paid $6,124,858 from the Broadway production alone. But Hal Prince is an important "name" director who probably negotiated a higher royalty rate, perhaps as much as 2 percent or 3 percent of gross receipts, which would amount to $25 million to $33 million. And the Broadway royalty doesn't include his royalties from productions of *Phantom* all over the world, including the productions touring the United States and the one running in a Las Vegas casino-hotel, plus whatever share of the movie sale Prince was entitled to in his contract.

There is only one Prince and only one *Phantom.* One can hardly plan a career based on these kind of extraordinary returns. As with actors, stars matter in directing, playwriting, composing, and design.

Some union minimums in table 3 may seem adequate in themselves, but theater artists are limited in the number of jobs they can attract and perform in a year. One Los Angeles-based theater director said, "In my very best year, I made just over $55,000. And I practically killed myself to do it."

Consider yearly earnings for an imaginary director who directs four LORT C shows in a year; that director would be paid a total of $31,400. A scenic designer with four LORT C shows in a year would end up with a total of $12,044, and a lighting designer, a total of $9,832. An actor who gets twenty-six weeks' work a year with a LORT C company at the minimum union rate of $696 per week thus receives a total of $18,096, while an actor at a LORT A company at minimum rates gets a total of $22,490 for working twenty-six weeks.

American Theatre reported in 2001 that 75 percent of working scenic designers also teach. Teaching gives them a secure wage and benefits.

When examining union minimums for directors and designers there are two important considerations: the payment based on the theater's classification and the number of shows a theater professional can be hired to perform to add up to a yearly wage

The International Alliance of Theatrical Stage Employees (IATSE) has many different locals around the country, representing workers in a number of theater and theater-related fields, such as film and television. A list of all types of workers covered in IATSE locals can be found in appendix C. When IATSE locals are listed in this chapter, we are referring only to theater locals. In a few cases—but especially in the case of the stagehands union—there are locals in more than one city.

The cities and local numbers for the stagehands unions are listed in appendix D. In this chapter, we refer only to New York City IATSE locals.

International Alliance of Theatrical Stage Employees (IATSE)
Local 829, United Scenic Artists

United Scenic Artists is a labor union and professional association of designers, artists, and craftspeople working in film, theater, opera, ballet, television, industrial shows, commercials, and exhibitions.

Membership

The information that follows was in effect in March 2011. Local USA 829 currently admits members into the following categories of membership for theater workers:

> Scenic artist—lay-out, surface decoration, sculpting, mold making, casting and painting of scenery and properties, building models and miniatures;
> Scenic designer—design, sketching, drafting, model building, and supervision of scenery;
> Costume designer—design, selection, painting, and dyeing of costumes;
> Lighting designer—design and direction of lighting;
> Sound designer—create the aural environment including sound effects and music;
> Projection designer—design of projections for all media;
> Computer artist;
> Allied crafts—this category includes costume painters; no new members are being accepted into this category;
> Industrial member—assists the scenic artist in scenic shops.

If hired by a union employer, an artist may apply for membership and in some cases is required to do so. All scenic artists applying as professional members must present their portfolio for review by a scenic artist review committee. The review process tests specific skills. According to United Scenic Artists publications, experience in the profession is the best preparation, and applicants from academic or fine arts backgrounds are encouraged to work in the field before applying to the union.

Fees and Dues

The initiation fee is $3,500 plus IATSE dues and fees totaling approximately $300. Industrial members pay an initiation fee of $250. Dues are 2 percent of gross wages.

Benefits

Local 829 provides access to health insurance and retirement benefits for some members through employer contributions of pension, welfare, 401(k), and other annuity benefits.

IATSE Local 18032, Association of
Theatrical Press Agents and Managers

ATPAM represents press agents, publicity and marketing specialists, company managers, and house and facilities managers. The information that follows was in effect as of January 2011.

Membership

Any press agent or manager engaged under the terms of an ATPAM agreement is eligible to join. A nonmember apprentice manager (*NMAM*) may be employed when hired under the minimum basic agreement (MBA) between ATPAM and the producer. The NMAM must pay a nonrefundable registration fee of $250. To be eligible for membership in the union, NMAM candidates must accumulate at least 52 credit weeks on valid contracts over a period of not less than two and not more than three consecutive seasons. No fewer than 10 credit weeks must be accumulated in each season, and no more than 42 credit weeks may be accumulated in one season. Any NMAM who fails to complete the program within three consecutive seasons shall be removed from the program. Following accumulation of 52 credit weeks, all NMAMs must pass an oral and written test for union admission.

Fees and Dues

The initiation fee is $2,000, plus an application processing fee of $100. Annual dues for membership are $200. Depending on the contract, members pay 3 to 3.25 percent of their gross salary in working dues.

Benefits

ATPAM provides comprehensive health insurance (after meeting eligibility requirements), pension plans, and credit union membership if desired.

IATSE Local 306, Audio/Visual Operators

Local 306 provides audio/visual workers for trade shows, seminars, conferences, concerts, and theater. In addition to A/V workers, it covers ticket takers, ushers, and doormen. It had 105,180 members as of January 2011, not all of them working in the legitimate theater. According to the 2009 Local 306 filing with the U.S. Department of Labor, yearly fees were $36 to $54, working dues were 2 percent to 4 percent of gross income, and initiation fees were $80 to $1,000.

IATSE Local 1, Theatrical Stage Employees

Local 1 represents stagehands in theater and in other presenting venues in New York City. It has a little more than 3,000 members. The local's Department of Labor filing for 2009 shows working dues of 4 percent of gross wages with an initiation fee of $500 to $2,000. (For a listing of IATSE Stage Employee locals for other areas, see appendix D.)

Local 1 publishes little information for nonmembers about how to join the union. When the stagehand union went on strike over proposed changes to work rules in November 2007, some information was released. The community of stagehands has been described as insular. James J. Claffey Jr., the president of the stagehands union during the 2007 Broadway strike, is one of six brothers, all union stagehands, according to the *New York Times*. Claffey became a stagehand the day after he graduated from high school in 1982; he was following his father's profession. That route to union membership is said to be typical, as sons have followed their fathers into the stagehand union for generations, and now daughters may well follow their fathers or mothers into the profession.

Earnings of Stagehands and Other Backstage Workers

Roughly 350 to 500 union stagehands work in the Broadway theater at any given time. The stagehands' union doesn't publicize minimum salaries for Broadway or elsewhere. However, when Local One went on strike some information was given to the press. Broadway union stagehands fall into four wage categories. At the top are head carpenters and electricians, then paid a minimum of $1,600 a week on a running show, a yearly salary of $83,200. Stagehands in the lowest category were paid a minimum of about $1,225, or $63,700 yearly. A stagehand with a long-running Broadway show may work all year. And with overtime and other premium assignments, wages can end up being quite a bit higher.* One assumes that stagehands in less lucrative venues than the Broadway theater are paid less than these rates and nonunion stagehands even less.

---

* There are better paying gigs than Broadway. Bloomberg.com reported in October 2009 that the stagehand who oversees props at New York's Carnegie Hall, the famous concert venue, made $530,044 in salary and benefits during 2008. The four other members of the full-time stage crew had an average income of $430,543 during the same period. These salaries included significant hours of overtime. The stagehands move equipment in and out of the hall, prepare the three stages for performances, and operate audiovisual and sound equipment. Source: Bloomberg.com, http://www.bloomberg.com/apps/news?pid= newsarchive&sid=agzioCanEd0s. Accessed June 2011.

IATSE Local 798, Make-up Artists and Hairstylists

Local 798 represents make-up artists and hairstylists in theater and in other presenting venues. It has a little more than 1,300 members. Local 798 publishes little information for nonmembers to give specifics of how one becomes a member or what the fees and dues of membership are. In their 2003 filing with the U.S. Department of Labor, the local reported that regular fees were $100 yearly and initiation fees ran from $1,500 to $3,000.

IATSE Local 764, Wardrobe Personnel

Local 764 represents wardrobe supervisors (or costumers) and assistants. Its total membership is 1,149, which includes workers in venues other than theater. Securing work is the only method of gaining membership. The union fees are $49 yearly plus working dues of 2 percent of gross wages. The initiation fee is $1,000.

IATSE Local 751, Treasurers and Ticket Sellers Union

Local 751 represents box office staff and management. It reported 492 members in its 2010 Department of Labor filing. Requirements for membership are not published. The union fees are $72 yearly. Initiation fee is $1,500.

Beyond the Facts

The facts about theatrical unions are important to know when beginning a theater career. For many outside the professions, membership in a theatrical union is the essence of professionalism. Still there are many people successfully working in theater who are not union members. The question is, "How central are unions to the career of a theater professional?" Few high school teachers or counselors know much about theatrical unions. Few if any undergraduate drama courses introduce current information about the main theatrical unions outlined in this chapter.

Unions are bureaucratic entities dominated by rules: rules for employers, rules for members, and rules for outsiders seeking membership. Gaining membership in some unions is relatively easy, but for others the path to union membership is difficult or obscure or both. For at least one theater union, it seems the most common way to join is to inherit the opportunity from a relative who already belongs to the union.

Beyond the facts lie opinions. Here are some of ours. We believe that unions fulfill an important societal function, but we also believe that given the structure of theater unions and the availability of jobs today, union membership is not a prerequisite for a theater career. Unions' marketing materials usually stress that their members are professionals. And they are professionals in the sense that they belong to the professional union in their field. However, to lack union membership does not preclude being a professional in one's approach to work and craft. Nor does not being a union member prevent finding work in professional theaters that do not require union membership.

United Scenic Artists advises recent graduates to gain professional experience before applying for membership. Casting agents and some theater teachers advise actors to do the same. We agree. As difficult as a student may find classes and artistic work in a college or university, the professional life is even more challenging. At least the student who gets work before joining a professional union will be able to know through personal experience what the value of union membership is.

CHAPTER 6

Theater Jobs Are Everywhere . . . but Mostly in New York

Sometimes facts bolster common wisdom. The widespread advice for people looking for theater jobs is, "go to New York City." Sometimes the counsel might add Chicago, San Francisco, or Seattle. Folks who follow theater know these cities are hotbeds of theatrical activity. But these same theater professionals also know that jobs for the full array of employment opportunities identified in chapter 1 can be found all over the United States. This chapter will focus on employers and the jobs they create, either in commercial or not-for-profit theaters.

The job facts presented here come mostly from information developed by the federal government's economic census and its employment surveys. These reports identify many of the concentrations of theater jobs in the United States. Information about jobs is also available from some theatrical unions and other organizations.

Theater Employers

The American Community Survey (ACS) of the U.S. Census estimates the number of employers, including theater employers, their revenues, payrolls, and number of employees. Only entities with one or more employees are included. From this ACS sample and by using other population data, the census extrapolates the survey data to estimate totals for the entire population.

One category the ACS tracks is "Theatre companies and dinner theaters." The definition of "theatre companies" includes musicals and plays plus operas, comedy acts, and mime and puppet shows. Specifically not included are nightclubs, presenters that do not produce their shows, dance companies, freelance producers and performers, and musicians and vocalists.

This definition is not perfectly suited to the kind of theater that concerns us here. It is, however, as close to a measure of legitimate theater as is found in the national statistics. (*Legitimate theaters* refers to those presenting plays and musicals. The term dates back to London in the early eighteenth century when a small number of theaters were licensed by the crown and thus "legitimate.")

Number of Theater Employers by State

Fig. 6. In general, the number of theater employers in a state is related to but not necessarily proportional to the population of the state. The states with the largest populations are California, Texas, New York, Florida, and Illinois. Only those five states have more than 145 theaters. Source: American Community Survey 2007

The greatest numbers of employers are in five densely populated states. No surprise there. They include California, Florida, Illinois, New York, and Texas. Together these states have over 3,423 theater employers (see fig. 6). To a great extent, the number of theaters correlates with overall population. The five states with the largest populations have the most theaters: California, Texas, New York, Florida, and Illinois. Together these states have nearly one-half of all theater employers in the United States. California and New York State have the greatest numbers of theater employers, with 620 and 452, respectively. The next largest number of theaters, 175, is found in Florida. These figures sometimes translate into lots of jobs.

The second group of states, those with between 50 and 144 employers, represent 1,131 theaters. Those with between 25 and 49 employers cover 406 employers. The final two categories represent 322 employers.

But although these employers have at least one employee, some employers may be, at heart, largely volunteer amateur organizations. These community-type theaters may employ a secretary, a bookkeeper, or a janitor, but they may or may not pay actors, directors, designers, or those who tech their productions.

Number of Theater Employees by State

Fig. 7. The states with a high number of employer theaters generally have a high number of theater employees. Some states with small samples were not reported because to do so might violate the confidentiality of the survey. Source: American Community Survey 2007.

Which of the ACS-identified theaters employ people other than managerial staff is unknown.

Employees

California, Texas, New York, Florida, and Illinois also have the most theater employees according to the ACS, with more than 33,750 total.

New York, an extrapolated 13,456 theater employees
California, 10,486
Illinois, 3,745
Florida, 3,386
Texas, 2,684

The total number of theater jobs in the United States, as provided by the ACS, is 69,174 (see fig. 7.)

How much do these employees earn? The answers may be surprising. Calculating average salary per theater employee from the census survey data shuffles the state rankings. Average salary per employee was calculated by dividing total payroll by the total number of employees. For theaters in the United States as a whole, the average salary is $28,844. The top seven states in terms of average payment per employee follow.

> Nevada ($59,001)
> Wyoming ($49,528)
> New York ($48,984)
> Connecticut ($30,961)
> Maine ($28,309)
> Illinois ($26,902)
> California ($26,191)

Nevada's top spot is not surprising. The state has a large number of entertainment venues connected to its hotel-casinos. Some significant number of these are not legitimate theaters but are counted in this ACS category. For example, the Cirque de Soleil shows in Las Vegas are counted in this category although their shows are variety shows, not theater per se. Nevada also has a long-standing high level of union membership; union membership generally increases an employee's salary.

Wyoming, however, is not a theater hotspot. The economic census projects that Wyoming has seven employer theaters with thirty-six salaried employees. Because the population in Wyoming is small and the sample is small as well, the extrapolation of the economic survey—using a small sample to estimate the state—is probably less reliable than in states with bigger samples. A search through the IRS 990 forms and Google reveals seven NFP theaters in Wyoming, of which only three list salaries as an expense. Those three theaters pay a substantial salary to their artistic director, executive director, and similar people, and little or nothing to other employees. Hence their average salary per employee is high. Another organization, the Jackson Hole Playhouse, is a dinner theater; its payroll is not publicly available.

New York City: The Center for Theater Jobs

If theaters are most likely to be found in states with larger populations, then it is to be expected that most theaters are in large urban areas. This assumption is borne out by the ACS results, with New York City claiming the most U.S. theater jobs. The Census Bureau, however, doesn't report on the jobs found just in city limits of New York, but also those in its environs.

The census almost always reports economic results not for cities but for core-based statistical areas (CBSAs). CBSAs are, by the U.S. Census definition, "at least one urbanized area of 50,000 or more population, plus adjacent territory that has a high degree of social and economic integration with the core as measured by commuting ties." The reason to use CBSAs instead of city limits is that these areas around cities are closely linked economically. In New York City, as an example, many people who work, shop, or attend theater in New York live in nearby cities and nonincorporated areas.

According to the Economic Census for 2002—census reports at the level of the CBSA were not available for the 2007 Economic Census as of March 2011— in the New York City–Newark, New Jersey–Bridgeport, Connecticut statistical area

> there were 607 employer theaters;
> 340 of these were commercial entities;
> 267 were not-for-profit.

A very great proportion of New York State theaters are in the New York City general area.

Many regional theaters—union and nonunion—audition actors in New York for major roles or review portfolios and conduct hiring interviews in New York to fill major design and technical positions. National touring companies fill acting and technical positions, both union and nonunion, out of New York City as well. This adds to the dominance of New York City as a job market for theater artists. To a lesser extent, regional theaters will hire in Los Angeles as well.

Broadway

Commercial theater in the United States is virtually confined to much of Broadway theater, some off-Broadway theater, much of theater touring, including long-staying productions in Las Vegas hotel-casinos, and a dwindling number of dinner theaters. (The National Dinner Theatre Association has twenty-four members. In the last 25 years, Actors' Equity reports weeks of work in the dinner theater for its members have declined by 65 percent.)

Used correctly, the term *Broadway* denotes theaters in midtown Manhattan that seat at least five hundred. Only productions in these theaters are eligible for Tony Awards. In 2011 there were forty Broadway theaters. Five are owned or controlled by not-for-profit theaters. Another not-for-profit theater, Second Stage, is planning to purchase the Helen Hayes Theatre; this acquisition will bring the number of not-for-profit Broadway theaters to six. Clearly, not-for-profit theaters are invading the commercial Broadway theater scene.

About one-quarter of new Broadway shows in recent seasons have been funded by not-for-profit entities. The remainder of Broadway shows are commercial. These commercial productions include a number of very long-running musicals, such as *The Phantom of the Opera, The Lion King, Wicked, Jersey Boys,* and *Chicago.*

Off-Broadway

There are about 130 productions off-Broadway each season. About one-quarter of these are commercial productions. Yet the exact number of off-Broadway commercial theaters is hard to quantify. The League of Off-Broadway Theatres and Producers (LOOBTOP) has nine member theaters. LOOBTOP lists another seventeen commercial theaters that are not members of the league; it makes no claim to having a complete list. Thus there are at least twenty-six commercial off-Broadway spaces compared with thirty-five commercial Broadway houses.

The average run of off-Broadway shows is between six and ten weeks. For comparison the average run for *new productions* on Broadway in the period from 1999 to 2000 through 2005–6 was 290 performances, or approximately 36 calendar weeks.

Off-Off-Broadway

Off-off-Broadway refers to productions in Manhattan theaters even smaller than off-Broadway theaters, theaters of ninety-nine or fewer seats. In early 2010 the website *Off-Off OnLine* (www.offoff-online.com) listed more than three hundred off-off-Broadway venues. Off-off-Broadway shows range from commercial and not-for-profit professional productions, both of which may be union or non-union, to amateur performances.

Some off-off-Broadway productions that cast members of Equity are called *Showcases*. Actors and stage managers under the Showcase Code are not required by their union to be paid except reimbursement for public transportation for rehearsals and performances. If the producer has a paying production later, there may be a contractual obligation to hire or pay Showcase actors. Total Showcase budgets can't exceed twenty thousand dollars; performances can't exceed twelve in four weeks; and ticket price can't exceed fifteen dollars. Still, in spite of the constraints, many Showcases are mounted; in 2007 Equity recorded 1,045 off-off-Broadway showcases.

Touring

The Broadway League producers send out tours of many of the shows they originated on Broadway. In the 2009–10 season, there were approximately forty Broadway League touring shows traveling across the country, playing in more than two hundred cities and with revenues greater than $947 million total.

Plays and musicals are also licensed to other producers for tours. Some non-league tours are national; some are regional. Most are commercial, and a few are not-for-profit. Many are union and some are not. Nonleague tours are estimated to have combined budgets of roughly one-half the budget of the Broadway League tours.

It's True: New York Has the Most Jobs

Because of the opportunities to work on Broadway, off Broadway, and off-off-Broadway and to be cast in a touring production, New York delivers the jobs. No wonder some advisers say, "Go to New York!"

Other Concentrations of Theaters and Jobs

The greatest number of theater productions in America are organized as not-for-profit (NFP) ventures. The census identified five states with large numbers of employer theaters, including Illinois and Texas. With few exceptions, these are NFP theaters.

In the 2008–9 season NFP theaters presented about seventeen thousand productions, with total budgets nationwide of $1.9 billion. These figures represent a lot of jobs, on stage, backstage, and in administration offices. The unanswerable question is how much of this activity is *professional* not-for-profit theater? There are NFP theaters that define themselves as amateur. These amateur theaters may have some paid personnel, such as executive directors, technical directors, secretaries, and box office staff. At the other end are theaters that engage solely union actors and other union personnel and thus are clearly professional. Between those extremes a clear meaning of "professional" is unclear. The largest organization for the professional NFP theater is the Theatre Communications Group (TCG). TCG has a membership of about 481 theaters nationwide. (See fig. 7.) This number does not include all professional NFP theaters.

An examination of some professional NFP theaters in two cities, the District of Columbia area, and one state indicates the opportunity to find work in theater is not limited to New York City.

Chicago, Illinois

Some savvy theater people advise novice theater artists to go to Chicago to seek their first theater jobs. Nicknamed "the Second City," Chicago is the most populous city in the Midwest and the third most populous city in the United States, with more than 2.8 million residents. Chicago actor and playwright Tracy Letts, author of *August: Osage County*, said, "Artists in Chicago are here to hone our craft and share our stories; audiences are adventurous and they appreciate new work. . . . The work is not precious or pretentious, and it is characteristic of a no-nonsense ethic that is an integral part of the warp and woof of Chicago."

The League of Chicago Theatres, a trade association, has 175 members; it includes presenters that are not producing legitimate theaters, such as circuses, cabarets, roadhouses, and dance and opera companies. Some forty Chicago theaters are bound by the Chicago Area Theaters contract with Equity. The League of Chicago Theaters calculated recently that there were approximately 800 productions in Chicago during the 2009–10 season, including more than 130 world premiere plays or adaptations.

Chicago union actors work more weeks per union member than elsewhere in the United States. During the 2005–6 season, Actors' Equity reported that its central region, which includes Chicago, accounted for 8.5 percent of its union members but 16.4 percent of workweeks.

Chicago's three LORT theaters are among its largest and most influential: the Goodman, the Northlight, and the Court. Other important Chicago theaters include Chicago Shakespeare Theatre and Victory Gardens Theatre. Perhaps Chicago's most influential theater is Steppenwolf Theater, which is not a member of LORT.

Theater Communications Group and LORT Members by State

Fig. 8. Members of these two organizations for professional NFP theaters are distributed much like all theater employers. Theater Communications Group members by state were extracted from the member profiles on the TCG site, which listed 304 members with profiles online (http://www.tcg.org/tools/profiles/member_profiles/main.cfm?CFID=27588281&CFTOKEN=66245604, accessed January 2011). This depiction of League of Resident Theatres by state was extracted from the member list on the LORT website (http://lort.web.officelive.com/members.aspx, accessed March 2011). A fuller description of LORT is found in a sidebar on page 21.

Throughout this chapter, basic information is given on a few of the largest theaters in the geographic area discussed, to offer an idea of the kinds of productions given, the number of jobs available, and the salaries involved.

Steppenwolf Theater. Since 1976 Steppenwolf has nurtured many important actors, including, Gary Sinise, John Malkovich, Laurie Metcalf, Terry Kinney, and others, and many playwrights, including Tracy Letts. Company members include Joan Allen, Kevin Anderson, John Mahoney, Martha Plimpton, Austin Pendleton, Lois Smith, and others. Several Steppenwolf productions have toured widely to great acclaim, including *True West, Grapes of*

from the Steppenwolf IRS filing 2008

Budget: $13 million
Artistic Director: $229,457
Executive Director: $229,546
Director of Development: $117,387
Director of Marketing: $113,342
Other salaries and wages: $5.5 million.

Wrath, and *August: Osage County.* The company describes itself as follows: "Committed to the principle of ensemble performance through the collaboration of a company of actors, directors and playwrights, Steppenwolf Theatre Company's mission is to advance the vitality and diversity of American theater by nurturing artists, encouraging repeatable creative relationships and contributing new works to the national canon."

Steppenwolf's 2010–11 season included four premiere productions, revivals of *Who's Afraid of Virginia Woolf?* and *The Hot L Baltimore*, productions of two recent plays premiered elsewhere, and two productions for young adults. It showcased work by other Chicago NFP theaters, including *Sonnets for an Old Century*, by the UrbanTheater Company; *The Three Faces of Doctor Crippen,* by the Strange Tree Group; and *Heddatron* by Sideshow Theatre Company.

On its website in March 2011, Steppenwolf listed 43 ensemble members. Ensemble members are artists—actors, writers, designers, directors—who are involved in artistic management of Steppenwolf. No total number of employees could be found. We estimate Steppenwolf's staff to be about 450.

The Goodman Theatre. Founded in 1925, the Goodman Theatre claims to be Chicago's oldest and largest not-for-profit theater. It has received the Special Tony Award for Outstanding Regional Theatre, given by the Broadway League and the American Theatre Wing. Its mission statement, in part, reads, "By dedicating itself to three guiding principles—quality, diversity, and community—Goodman Theatre seeks to be the premier cultural organization in Chicago, providing productions and programs that make an essential

from the Goodman IRS filing 2007

Budget: $19.7 million
Artistic Director: $355,000
Executive Director: $326,397
General Manager: $208,800
Marketing Director: $143,100
Development Director: $143,100
Associate General Manager: $125,000
Associate Producer: $115,000
Other salaries and wages: $7.1 million.

contribution to the quality of life in our city." Directors staging plays at the Goodman include its artistic director Robert Falls, Mary Zimmerman, and Regina Taylor. Two revivals transferred to Broadway runs and received Tony Awards: *Death of a Salesman* (1999) and *Long Day's Journey into Night* (2002). It has premiered new work too, including the musicals *The Visit* and *The House of Martin Guerre* and plays such as *Marvin's Room, The Notebooks of Leonardo da Vinci,* and *Zoot Suit,* and many plays by August Wilson, David Mamet, and Rebecca Gilman.

The Goodman's 2010–11 season included productions of new plays including *Stage Kiss,* by Sarah Ruhl; *Chinglish,* by David Henry Hwang; *Mary,* by Thomas Bradshaw; *El Nogalar,* by Tanya Saracho; *God of Carnage,* by Yasmina Reza; and an evening of one-acts by Regina Taylor; it also presented revivals of *The Seagull* and the musical *Candide* and a production of *A Christmas Carol.*

In an annual report the Goodman listed 610 staff and artists working for the theater in the year ending August 31, 2005. These staff included officers, artists, part-time consultants, interns, and four custodians.

The Court Theatre. A professional theater on the grounds of the University of Chicago, the Court Theatre has a mission "to discover the power of classic theatre." It was founded in 1955 as an amateur outdoor summer theater, becoming a professional company in 1985. Its 2010–11 season included revivals of *The Comedy of Errors; Three Tall Women; Home,* by Samm-Art Williams; and *Porgy and Bess.* It also presented *Orlando,* a new adaptation by Sarah Ruhl of the Virginia Woolf novella.

The Court Theater Fund is a 501(c)(3) NFP corporation, but all income and expenditures are handled through the University of Chicago so budget information for the theater separate from the university's budget is not available. According to its posting at the Theatre Communications Group (TCG), the Court's 2010–11 budget was $3.4 million.

Northlight Theatre. Founded in 1974 and presently located in Skokie, a suburb of Chicago, Northlight Theatre writes of its mission that it "aspires to promote change of perspective and encourage compassion by exploring the depth of our humanity across a bold spectrum of theatrical experiences. [It seeks] to entertain, enlighten, and electrify [its] audiences through contemporary dra-

from the Northlight IRS filing 2008

Budget: $3.1 million
Artistic Director: $106,777
Executive Director: $95,393
Other salaries and wages: $645,399

mas, intimate musicals and refreshed classics. [It is] fearless in [its] commitment to champion new work, and to provide a nurturing and creative home for . . . artists."

The Northlight's 2010–11 season included a joint production with Cincinnati's Playhouse in the Park of a new musical *Daddy Long Legs*; Paula Vogel's play *A Civil War Christmas; Eclipsed,* by Danai Gurira; and two world premieres, *The Outgoing Tide,* by Bruce Graham; and a new adaptation of Jane Austen's novel *Sense and Sensibility.*

Northlight's website in March 2011 listed 18 staff members. We estimate the total staff to number about fifty.

Chicagoland has at least three more large not-for-profit theaters that are not members of LORT: Chicago Shakespeare Theater, Victory Gardens Theater, and Writers' Theatre.

Chicago Shakespeare Theater. This theater performs mostly the plays of Shakespeare and is the 2008 recipient of the Regional Theatre Tony Award. It had a budget in excess of $12.5 million as of its 2008 IRS report. Officers and key staff were paid a total of $724,292. Other salaries and wages totaled somewhat more than $4.8 million. Its website in March 2011 listed 147 staff, not counting actors.

Victory Gardens Theater. Considered a playwrights' theater. At Victory Gardens Theater's heart is a "playwrights ensemble" with fourteen members, and it has received the Regional Theatre Tony Award. It reported a budget of less than $3.4 million in 2008. Key officers were paid $181,993, with $1,291,688 in other salaries and wages. Its March 2011 website listed forty-one on staff, not counting actors.

Writers' Theatre. Founded in 1994, the Writers' Theatre in the Chicago suburb of Glencoe states that the text on the page, both contemporary and classic, is its highest value. Its 2008 IRS filing shows a budget of a little more than $3.3 million. Executive compensation was $248,424; other salaries and wages were more than $1.3 million. Not counting actors, Writer's Theatre staff totaled thirty-eight, according to its website as of March 2011.

Texas

Texas is the second-largest U.S. state by both area and population and has the fifth largest number of employer theaters, 156, per the U.S. Economic Census. Two cities in Texas rank in the top ten in the United States in population, with Houston the fourth largest and San Antonio the seventh largest. In terms of CBSA metropolitan areas, Dallas–Fort Worth and Greater Houston are the fourth and sixth largest in the United States, respectively.

Texas has two LORT theaters, the Alley Theatre and the Dallas Theater Center. Four more theaters have annual budgets in excess of $1 million a year. (These large theaters were identified through the membership rolls at Theatre

Communications Group. There may be other large theaters in Texas that are not members of TCG.)

The Alley Theatre. Located in Houston, this theater is among the oldest not-for-profit professional theaters in the United States, begun by Nina Vance in 1947 and becoming a professional company in 1954. The Alley declares that it "is one of the few American Theatre companies that supports a company of actors, designers, artisans and craftspeople throughout the year." Using actor biographies on the Alley's website as a source, we found that the Alley has a core of actors it hires repeatedly. It produces on two stages, the 824-seat Hubbard and the

from the Alley IRS filing 2008

Budget: $15.8 million
Artistic Director: $303,261
Managing Director: $285,704
Finance Director: $91,442
General Manager: $101,819
Director of Communications: $101,467
Director of Development: $135,417
Other salaries and wages: $6.2 million

310-seat Neuhaus, and presents about eleven productions each season. Its mission "is to deepen the understanding of ourselves, one another, and the world we share by uniting theatre artists and audiences to experience the power of stories that illuminate the breadth and complexities of the human condition."

The Alley's 2010–2011 season included stagings of three recent New York successes, two revivals, two world premiere plays, a children's play, and two Christmas productions, one aimed at the whole family (a new version of Dickens' *A Christmas Carol*) and one aimed at adults (David Sedaris's one-person *The Santaland Diaries.*)

The Alley has a core acting company of 9, hiring additional actors as needed, plus 126 employees, according to its website in March 2011.

The Dallas Theater Center. Founded in 1959, the Dallas Theater Center recently moved to a new performing space, the AT&T Performing Arts Center, from its original home, the Kalita Humphreys Theater, a theater designed by the architect Frank Lloyd Wright. Its mission statement maintains that the Dallas Theater Center "engages, entertains and inspires a diverse community by creating experiences that

from the Dallas Theater Center IRS filing 2009

Budget: $5.8 million
Artistic Director: $22,188
Managing Director: $19,610
Other salaries and wages: $240,000

stimulate new ways of thinking and living by consistently producing plays, educational programs and community initiatives that are of the highest quality and reach the broadest possible constituency." The Dallas Theater Center had an acting company of nine plus fifty-nine employees as of March 2011, according to its website.

The Dallas Theater Center's 2010–11 season included a Shakespeare play, one world-premiere play, two musicals in revival (*The Wiz* and *Cabaret*), a recently successful Broadway play (*Dividing the Estate*), an old chestnut (*Arsenic and Old Lace*), and the perennial *A Christmas Carol*.

WaterTower Theatre. Three of the four next largest by budget theaters in Texas are in Houston, and the fourth, the WaterTower Theater, is in Addison, a suburb of Dallas.

from the WaterTower IRS filing 2009

Budget: $1.3 million
Executive Director: $84,000
Other salaries and wages: $614,869

For more than fifteen years, the Water-Tower Theatre has presented professional theater in Addison. At present it produces five shows a season. Its mission is "to open minds with a diverse mix of plays and educational programs that inspire people to experience and embrace live theatre." The 2010–11 season included *Our Town, Circle Mirror Transformation, The Little Shop of Horrors, The Lieutenant of Inishmore*, a little-known Horton Foote play, and a new play by Steven Dietz. WaterTower's staff numbers twelve, not including actors.

Main Street Theater. The mission of Main Street Theater is "to create theater that challenges its audience to think and its artists to grow . . . by presenting an articulate and compelling product in an intimate setting, creating significant employment for Houston-based artists, and memorable theatrical experiences for audiences of all ages." It presents in two spaces, one with 250 seats

from the Main Street Theater
IRS filing 2008

Budget: $1.4 million
Executive Director: $40,000
Other salaries and wages: $463,645

and a second with 92. Its main stage 2010–11 season included Shaw's *The Doctor's Dilemma, The Heidi Chronicles, A Catered Affair* (a musical), *The Year of Magical Thinking, Blithe Spirit*, and a new play by Melissa James Gibson. Its New/Now series presented two world premieres and a regional premiere. Main Street Theater staff totals fifteen, not counting actors.

The Ensemble Theatre. Founded in 1976 to promote African American theater, the Ensemble produces a season of six contemporary and classical works in Houston for an audience that is 90 percent African American. It claims to be "the oldest and largest professional African American theatre in the Southwest, and holds the distinction of being one of the nation's largest African American theatres owning and operating its facility." Its 2010–11 season included *Gee's Bend; Jitney,* by August Wilson; *Hi-Hat Hattie: The Story of Hattie McDaniel; No Child; Blues in the Night;* Samm-Art Williams's *The Waiting Room;* and *The African American Shakespeare Company's Cinderella.* The Ensemble has a staff of nine, not counting actors.

*from the Ensemble Theatre
IRS filing 2009*

Budget: $1.8 million
Executive Director: $74,429
Artistic Director: $73,820
Other salaries and wages: $501,289

Stages Repertory. This repertory theater states that it "produces new work, interprets established work in new ways, and nurtures talent to invigorate culture for the good of the community." It was founded in Houston in 1978. Its 2010–11 season included *The Marvelous Wonderettes, Auntie Mame, Oh the Humanity, Yankee Tavern, Four Places, The Great American Trailer Park Musical,* and a premiere family musical, *Panto Pinocchio.* Staff numbers are not available for Stages Repertory.

Washington, D.C.

The 2008 American Community Survey shows fifty-three theater and dinner theater employers in the Washington, D.C., statistical area, which includes Arlington and Alexandria, Virginia. Twenty-five of those theaters report hiring between one and four employees. The average salary per employee was $25,076. There are eight theaters in the District of Columbia that are members of TCG and three that are members of LORT. At least six D.C. theaters have budgets in excess of $1 million.

Shakespeare Theatre. First housed in the Folger Library's theater, the Shakespeare Theatre performed on an approximation of an Elizabethan outdoor stage. The company has grown and prospered over the years, and in 2007 it completed a new theater, the Harman Center for the Arts. The mission of the Shakespeare Theatre is to become the nation's premier classic theatre. By focusing on works with profound themes, complex characters, and heightened language written by Shakespeare, his contemporaries and those playwrights he influenced, the Shakespeare Theatre Company is unique among regional theaters in

*from the Shakespeare Theatre
IRS filing 2008*

Budget: $22 million
Artistic Director: $346,618
Managing Director: $138,368
Chief Development Officer: $180,909
Director of Production: $103,833
Director of Administration: $103,800
Managing Director: $100,500
Other salaries and wages: $7.8 million

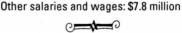

its mission to bring to vibrant life groundbreaking, thought-provoking and eminently accessible classic theater in a uniquely American style.

For more than twenty years, the Shakespeare Theatre has fulfilled its mission. It produces about seven shows a year, mostly Shakespeare's or other classic plays of language. With its recently built theater complex, the Shakespeare Theatre invites other local, national, or international theater and dance troupes to be showcased on its stages. It also has an extensive education department. According to its annual report for 2010, theater staff totals 394, not counting actors except for those who are teaching artists or interns. The Shakespeare Theatre Company is a member of LORT.

Incidentally the Folger Shakespeare Library in which the Shakespeare Theatre originated is home to perhaps the world's largest and finest collection of Shakespeare materials and to other Renaissance books, manuscripts, and works of art. Since the Shakespeare Theatre left the facility, a second company has been created there, called the Folger Theatre. It mounts three productions each season, mostly of Shakespeare. The theater is connected to the library and does not submit IRS filings on its own. Its budget according to the Theatre Communications Group is $1.2 million.

Ford's Theatre Society. This theater is a national park, preserving and interpreting the site where President Lincoln was assassinated in 1865. Ford's Theatre Society has been presenting plays in the theater since 1968. It generally produces four shows in addition to hosting some touring events and television specials, as well as its annual *A Christmas Carol.* The society also presents a one-act play on a regular schedule as part of the National Park Service's interpretation of the site for visitors. Ford's Theatre Society has a staff of 75, with a great part of the budget going to contractors for design, construction, and stage equipment.

Arena Stage. Among the earliest NFP theaters in the United States, the Arena Stage was founded in 1950. It was also the first NFP theater to transfer a production to Broadway, 1968's *The Great White Hope.* It has developed another fourteen productions that went on to Broadway runs. In 2011 it reopened a renovated theater complex with three stages under one roof. Its regular season includes eight plays. In 2011–12

from the Arena Stage (Washington Drama Society) IRS filing 2008

Budget: $14.3 million
Artistic Director: $235,754
Interim Managing Director: $151,174
Other salaries and wages: $5 million

it planned to stage three shows in its new smallest theater, the Kogod Cradle. In addition to the artistic and managing directors, the Arena Stage has a staff totaling 179, not including actors. The employees are divided into seven departments:

17 in administration;

17 in artistic development, including five playwrights;

59 in communications;

9 in community engagement;

13 in development;

10 in operations;

54 in production.

In addition the Arena Stage has commissioned seven playwrights in addition to those employed in artistic development, and it is a member of LORT.

Signature Theatre. Arlington's Signature Theatre is focused on musical theater, new shows and imaginative restagings of past shows. It also stages non-musical plays; for example, in 2010 it staged the one-person show, *I Am My Own Wife.* A season is typically seven shows. It lists a staff of ninety-three, which includes some commissioned writers and recipients of grants for musical artists that are distributed through the Signature, but it doesn't include actors. Signature is a member of LORT. Signature also has an emphasis on education, operating a school for actors and free performances in the public schools. (New York City has a NFP theater also named Signature Theatre. The two groups are not related.)

from the Signature Theatre I
RS filing 2008

Budget: $9.4 million

Artistic Director: $137,298

Managing Director: $120,000

Other salaries and wages: $2.7 million

Studio Theatre. In Studio Theatre's four performing spaces—the largest seats 225—contemporary and innovative work is performed. The theater also has a focus on training young people in the arts. A season is typically nine productions; some are world premieres, others recent plays from the country's other regional theaters. In 2011 it also hosted a three-show festival of the plays of Irish playwright Enda Walsh, author of *The Walmouth Farce* and other plays. Studio lists eighty-three staff members, not including actors. It is not a member of LORT.

from the Studio Theatre IRS
filing 2008

Budget: $4.8 million

Artistic Director: not available in this filing. Salary in the 2005 filing was $106,022

President: $114,906

Vice President: $93,004

Secretary: $84,816

Other salaries and wages: $1.9 million

Wooly Mammoth Theatre Company. Founded in 1980, Wooly Mammoth Theatre Company serves "an essential 'Research and Development' role within the American theatre and plays premiered [there] have gone on to productions at more than 200 theatres in 39 states and 12 countries." A typical season includes six productions, some portion of those one-person shows. Staff totals thirty-eight, and the company lists an acting troupe of twenty-two. Wooly Mammoth is not a LORT theater.

from the Wooly Mammoth Theatre Company IRS filing 2008

Budget: $3.3 million
Artistic Director: $87,083
Managing Director: $81,175
Other salaries and wages: $1.2 million

Equity Jobs and Their Locations

Equity publications reinforce the Economic Census findings. Most Equity members—63 percent of union stage actors and stage managers—reside in what Equity defines as its eastern region. The western region houses 28 percent. Only 9 percent live in the central region. (See fig. 9 for the makeup of the Equity regions.) The top five cities in terms of percentage of Equity members are

> New York City, almost 39 percent;
> Los Angeles, 17.4 percent;
> Chicago, 3.4 percent;
> San Francisco, 2.2 percent;
> D.C. and Baltimore area, 2 percent.

Of course, these cities have actors and other theater artists who are not members of a union. In fact, as noted earlier, outside of New York and Los Angeles theater professionals may face a dilemma regarding union membership: with union membership salaries are higher but there are fewer union jobs available in many areas of the United States.

Other Unions and Locations

There are no statistics generally available from the other theater artists' unions like those that Equity publishes. The location and number of contracts the unions have negotiated with theaters give a notion of where jobs are located. In addition to LORT theaters which are nationwide, the contracts cluster in New York, Chicago, and to some extent, Washington, DC.

Equity Regions

Fig. 9. Equity divides its membership into three regions.

United Scenic Arts, IATSE Local 829

United Scenic Artists Local 829, the branch of the International Alliance of Theatrical Stage Employees (IATSE) representing stage designers and crafts people, also has three regions, but it does not publish member workweeks. Its only negotiated contract on a national basis is with the League of Resident Theatres (LORT).

Local 829 theater designers' contracts in the eastern region are with

Broadway theaters;
Papermill Playhouse (N.J.);
the Kennedy Center (D.C.), which produces theater, opera, music, and
    dance and serves as a booking house for touring shows of those four
    genres;
scenic suppliers in New York, Connecticut, Pennsylvania and Florida;
    the Independent Not-For-Profit Theaters Agreement (INTA).

INTA covers 27 theaters mostly in the Washington, D.C., area, including the Folger Shakespeare Library, Maryland Shakespeare Festival, Signature Theatre Company in D.C., and the Washington Stage Guild.

The central region covers scenic suppliers and shops in Chicago and St. Louis, and also

the Court and Victory Gardens Theatres in Chicago;
Municipal Theatre Association of St. Louis;
the Starlight Theatre, Kansas City.

The western region contracts include

the Ahmanson Theatre in Los Angeles;
the Marin Theatre Company and the Magic Theatre in the San Francisco
    Bay area;
the Foothill Theater Company (Calif.);
Seattle Children's Theatre.

Stage Directors and Choreographers Society

The Stage Directors and Choreographers Society (SDC)—the union representing directors and choreographers—has contracts for

Broadway League producers and Broadway League-originated tours;
the League of Off-Broadway Theatres and Producers which covers commercial and not-for-profit theaters of 100–500 seats in New York City;
LORT;
Council of Resident Stock Theatres concerning summer stock productions
    in four theaters in Maine, Pennsylvania, and Maryland;
Association of Non Profit Theatre Companies for nine theaters operating
    separately and independently within the five boroughs of New York City,
    including Classic Stage Company, Vineyard Theatre Company, Primary
    Stages, and others;
Regional Musical Theatre regarding Civic Light Opera-type theaters of
    unknown number;
Dinner theaters, of which there are only two signatories;
Outdoor musical theaters, which include four entities in St. Louis, Atlanta,
    Dallas, and Kansas City.

Additionally the SDC promulgates an agreement to be used by its members for commercial productions in theaters outside New York City that seat 100–499.

The negotiated contracts with the directors and choreographers union and the stage designers union are not the only places that union workers find employment, but they suggest that, for union theater artists in these disciplines, the bulk of jobs are in New York or in cities on the East Coast.

Beyond the Facts

It's true. The most number of theater jobs are in New York City or are filled from auditions and portfolio reviews held in New York. But there are other centers for theater jobs, generally in any city with a significant population base—Los Angeles, Chicago, Minneapolis/St. Paul—or in densely populated states—Florida, Texas.

No matter the geographic location, only NFP theaters with a significant budget size—more than $1 million—pay much to theater workers, although some smaller entities do provide living wages to their artistic directors or similar management positions.

However, those beginning a theater career may decide that a low-paying theater job is very much like an apprenticeship, where experience, understanding of the profession, and additional training may be acquired. Armed with the knowledge and experience from low- or no-pay engagements, one may find that a second job that is more financially rewarding is in the offing.

Beyond the facts lie opinion. Here are some of ours. We haven't mentioned theater and theater work at theme parks such as Disneyland or Six Flags over Texas (or Georgia) nor have we mentioned cruise lines. There's a reason for that omission. These are generally dead-end jobs. The work is fun no matter if you're a techie, in the cast of live show, or a "walk-around" character in a cartoon costume posing with customers. And the work pays. It's probably acceptable employment for a summer job while earning a B.A. degree. But cruise line and theme park work will not help a beginner build a respectable résumé. The same is probably true of work in the long-running outdoor historical pageants, such as *Unto these Hills* or *Tecumseh!* These engagements on a résumé will not impress a casting agent, producer, or artistic director.

An exception might be made for directors and writers working gigs for Disney cruise ships. Disney has hired rising young directors to develop shows for its ships. Diane Paulus, director of the recent Broadway revivals of *Hair* and *The Gershwins' Porgy and Bess,* was employed for a fifty-minute Disney cruise show in 2003. She spoke of the engagement with pride, saying, "I was used to working in downtown theater with [a budget of] $5,000, and suddenly I was working with several million dollars." Cruise ships are not a place for high-minded plays; as the *New York Times* wrote, "'Waiting for Godot' wouldn't work with a walk-on by Goofy." Still Disney hired Hunter Bell and Jeff Bowen, authors of the Broadway and off-Broadway post modern musical *[title of show]* to develop a cruise ship show titled "Villan Tonight!" that featured evil Disney characters.

CHAPTER 7

Real Theater Careers

Few careers in any discipline develop in a straight line. There may once have been a time when a person went to work for a company and stayed there to retirement. That's rare today. For most people a work life has second acts—and third acts. Perhaps more.

The ability to morph from one career path to another is pronounced in theater. Some of those who want a career as an actor, for example, may find themselves in a totally unrelated field years later. The same is true of those who want to be directors or designers. Perhaps one of the most telling examples of career shift was reported in *Dramatics*, published by the Educational Theatre Association, in a 2010 article, "30 Years On: Hofstra's Theatre Class of '79 Takes a Look Back." This particular drama class began with about fifteen aspirants eager for a theater education and perhaps a theater vocation.

Thirty years on, most of the Hofstra graduates are not connected with professional theater. Their present career paths include a couple of teachers; a chief talent officer at Young & Rubicam Brands in New York; an owner of a paralegal services company in Louisiana; a chief of an antinarcotics strike force in New York City; a litigation paralegal with a law firm in San Francisco; and a cofounder of a recording, reporting, and transcription company. In addition a couple are in general sales, a few participated in the creation of *Tony n' Tina's Wedding* (an Off-Broadway hit that opened in 1988 and was still running in early 2012), three are writers, another is a trial lawyer and author, and *one* is a regularly employed professional actor Off-Broadway and in regional theaters. Two had died. Clearly most of these theater hopefuls moved into new career paths, most not directly related with theater. Like the Hofstra group, many drama graduates trade their original career goals for other jobs.

Previous chapters focused on facts—statistics, averages, means, and other numerical evidence. This chapter takes a different approach. The facts about the careers of real people are told here in anecdotes and biographical sketches. These profiles are about people who were trained in theater—many beginning with the goal of being actors—who now work in theater but in ways they didn't imagine when they began.

Their brief stories illuminate how the discovery of other theater occupations emerged for specific individuals. One actor became a costume-shop supervisor, another a theater librarian, and yet another actor became a playwright. These individuals, and others, remain active in theater, but not in the career they first imagined they would have. It's not that they're disappointed; it's that as they learned more, they found other kinds of theater work that they liked more than their first choices. Their anecdotal tales expand the story of theater careers to give a personal face to some of the facts presented earlier.

These individuals are not celebrities like those covered by *Entertainment Tonight* on TV or *People* magazine. Information about the lives of superstars is widely available elsewhere. Besides, superstardom comes to such a small number of people that it can hardly offer a model or a goal for a beginner. If stardom comes, it comes like winning the lottery: a nice dream but not a feasible economic plan. We've also omitted the stories of many who just fell away from the theatre, became disgusted, embittered, and left for what they hoped were greener pastures. These disappointed people are many and, frankly, hard to locate. They've moved on.

Actor, Playwright

Matthew Lopez. Courtesy Old Globe, photograph by Jeffrey Weiser.

Matthew Lopez trained as an actor at the University of South Florida in Tampa. That's what he wanted to be. He graduated with a B.A. in 1998 and moved to New York in 2000. He auditioned for acting jobs but not much happened. Matthew now admits he was "not very good."

He turned to playwriting, his other love, to find his calling. His play *The Whipping Man* was developed in several not-for-profit theaters and made its way to New York as a production of the Manhattan Theatre Club in 2011, a top NFP theater, guided by a Tony Award–winning director and featuring first-rate actors. The designers for *The Whipping Man* were also A-list talents. Audiences liked it. The Manhattan Theatre Club extended the run three times. Lopez was 33 at the time.

So how did an untried playwright get a major production on the New York stage? Matthew has no formal training in playwriting. He refers to the development of *Whipping Man* at four regional theaters as his playwriting "graduate school."

Whipping Man began as a twenty-minute two-character sketch called "The Soldier and the Slave," written while Matthew was earning his living in various office jobs. A reader for a theater company thought "Soldier" had possibilities. Lopez developed the play over a two-year period, adding a third character in the process. Then, finally known as *The Whipping Man*, the much-revised play continued its development in regional productions, including Luna Stage, now in Philadelphia; Penumbra Theatre Company in Minnesota; the Old Globe in California; and Massachusetts's Barrington Stage. Through its various incarnations, *The Whipping Man* has garnered strong reviews and audience support. It won the John Gassner Playwriting Award given by the New York Outer Critics Circle.

The drama, set in 1865, is about a Jewish Confederate soldier who returns to find his family estate in ruins. The young man discovers two former slaves are still around, even though they have been emancipated. Both slaves were raised as Jews before the Civil War. The timing is significant. Just before the play begins, General Lee has surrendered at Appomattox and shortly thereafter Lincoln has been assassinated while attending a play at Ford's Theatre in Washington, D.C. During a Passover Seder dangerous secrets of the past are revealed that threaten the trio's family, their connected history, and their shared faith.

Matthew now has an agent and is a member of the Dramatists Guild of America. He has playwriting commissions from not-for-profit groups, including Roundabout Theatre Company, and the Old Globe. He is also a playwriting fellow with the New York Theatre Workshop.

Matthew is currently working on a play that also looks at history through the prism of outsiders. He calls it *Tio Pepe*. It's about a Puerto Rican family in the 1960s whose home is about to be torn down to make way for Lincoln Center. *Tio Pepe* was presented at the Public Theater in New York as part of the 2008 Summer Play Festival. He has two other plays in development: *Zoey's Perfect Wedding* and *Reverberation*.

When he was named playwright in residence at the Old Globe in 2010, its executive producer, Lou Spisto, described Matthew as "an emerging voice in the American theater. A fresh perspective and a narrative drive are the hallmarks of his developing talent." Matthew responded by noting, "I am at an exciting time in my career where the work I've done all these years is finally starting to be recognized and I am starting to be taken seriously as a writer. That feels good. If it doesn't exactly keep me in groceries, at least it keeps me in good spirits."

Librarian, Actor

Roderick Bladel started acting when he was nine years old; he played a cat in a school PTA production. Although Rod quips, "They never cast me again," others did. As an undergraduate at the University of California, Los Angeles (UCLA), he earned his Screen Actors Guild membership by acting small parts in two movies.

Later, while still a UCLA student, he was cast as the twelve-year-old juvenile in a West Coast tour of *The Happy Time*, a successful Broadway comedy by Samuel Taylor. Rod slyly said that he was cast "because of my talent and my youthful appearance." Part of that "appearance" was being short—5'4". He was a nineteen-year-old playing a character who was twelve years old.

Rod's acting career was off to a great start, but he found parts hard to come by; perhaps the problem in part was his slight stature. He turned to higher education. Rod completed an undergraduate degree at UCLA, earned a teacher's certificate at the University of Iowa, and an M.F.A. degree in acting from the Yale School of Drama. "I learned more about acting from Constance Welch in the three years I was at Yale," Rod notes. Later, he earned a doctorate in theater history at the University of Michigan. Finally, he completed a degree in library science.

While he has taught at the high school and university level, Rod's main career has been as a librarian at the New York Public Library Billy Rose Theatre Collection. With the security of a steady paycheck, Rod acted whenever the opportunities presented themselves. Using paid vacation leave, he has acted Off-Broadway, Off-Off-Broadway, and at regional theaters.

"The three favorite roles of my lifetime were all played by the time I was twenty-five years old," Rod fondly remembers. They were all in the amateur theater: Emil Bruckner in *Tomorrow the World* in high school; Marchbanks in *Candida* at UCLA; and Ensign Pulver in *Mister Roberts* at the University of Iowa. "No professional work has ever equaled the thrills I experienced as an amateur," Rod says. "Go figure!"

Rod has acted with Anne Jackson, Eli Wallach, James Dean, Charles Coburn, Billie Burke, Charles Kimbrough, and Wil Geer. He spent three seasons acting with the famed APA troupe (Association of Producing Artists), working with such luminaries as Ellis Rabb and Rosemary Harris. Rod is a member of Actors' Equity Association

He has never been a box-office name performer, but he has had a part-time stage career while earning his living as a theater librarian.

Lawyer, Company Manager, Broadway Substitute, Author

Tom Santopietro earned a degree in 1981 from the University of Connecticut School of Law but knew he would not be a lawyer. He jokes, "The American Bar Association is quite happy I am not practicing law—and I am equally happy." Instead he worked for more than twenty years as a company manager of more than thirty Broadway shows. Then he wrote books while temping as a substitute company manager or house manager. He's a Broadway pinch-hitter, still a member of the Association of Theatrical Press Agents and Managers, IATSE Local 18033.

Tom managed some important Broadway productions, including *Jersey Boys*, *A Few Good Men* (original production), *A Doll's House*, and *Noises Off* (original production). When there was a year-long period of unemployment in 1999, he hit on the idea of offering his services as a Broadway substitute. He filled in for company managers and house managers when they were on vacation or were pulled to other work. He found that he liked it.

Being a substitute gave him time to turn to writing. That turn was productive. He's researched and written three books, all published by St. Martin's Press. His first was about Barbra Streisand's performance career, and his second was on Doris Day. His latest, published in 2008, is *Sinatra in Hollywood*. He lectures and does cabaret based on his books.

The career path Tom Santopietro followed is unique—lawyer, company manager, Broadway pinch-hitter, and author. Tom proves here are many career paths in theater.

Stage Management on the Road, at a NFP Theater

For thirty years Matthew G. Marholin has been a production stage manager (PSM), the person in charge of everything backstage as well as the artistic integrity of a production once the director leaves. Stage managers and assistant stage managers report to the PSM. For example, on a national tour of *South Pacific*, Matt, as PSM, was the person who rehearsed Robert Goulet when, in 2002 at mid-tour, Goulet took over the leading role of Emile de Becque. As PSM, Matt "put in" the star replacement, working with Goulet on all the established staging and character work for that production. The director then came in for two rehearsals to complete the process.

Matt Marholin. Photograph courtesy of Samuel Flint

Matt was initiated into the art and craft of stage management as an undergraduate. Before earning a B.A. degree, he spent a summer as a stage manager for Green Mountain Guild (now called the Stowe Theatre Guild) in Vermont. After graduation he sought additional training as an apprentice stage manager with the Alliance Theatre in Atlanta. Matt earned membership in Actors' Equity Association, the professional union for stage managers, the next year while working with Theatre West Virginia in Beckley.

Armed with a union card, Matt worked around the country, Broadway, Off-Broadway, and internationally. For example, he was the production stage manager for a European tour of the musical *Carmen Jones,* Oscar Hammerstein II's adaptation of Bizet's opera *Carmen,* by the New York Harlem Theatre. His career took off. He became a sought after PSM for commercial productions on the road.

His *South Pacific* gig gave him employment for nearly a year. Another long-running gig was as PSM for a European tour of *Porgy and Bess,* the George Gershwin opera-musical. So was the national tour of *Camelot,* by Lerner and Loewe, and the first national tour of the Tony Award–winning musical *Urinetown.* In all Matt has guided about twenty national tours.

Perhaps Matt Marholin's most challenging professional assignment was as artistic director for a world tour of Cirque de Soleil's production of *Alegria.* Matt was responsible for the artistic quality of the production, scheduling performer-training sessions, overseeing the load-in and rigging for the production, and supervising the strike and load-out as well as reporting to Cirque headquarters in Montreal, Canada. The tour gave Matt six months' employment on the world stage.

"The road has lost its appeal for me," Matt concludes. "I am happier being stationed in one place with a not-for-profit theater company that produces a *season* of plays, not just one, make-or-break production. I realized that I could be just as proud of the product at a regional theater as I am of a high-tech, high-pressure commercial show. Additionally, I found that the security of continuous employment allows me to focus on each show rather than expending energy constantly looking for that next show. "To that end, he completed in 2012 his third year as the PSM for Virginia Stage Company in Norfolk. He is considering another career change. "I find very appealing the possibility of teaching what I have learned to theater students at the undergraduate or graduate level."

Theater Major, Theater Lawyer

Jean Ward graduated as a theater major from Beaver College in Pennsylvania (now Arcadia University). She believes theater can be "such a difficult, often discouraging career choice." Perhaps that's what led her to enter, and graduate from, Harvard Law School. After a stint with a corporate law firm, she moved into entertainment law at the invitation of another Harvard Law School graduate who was representing super-producer Cameron Mackintosh. Jean Ward loved the change. She now works exclusively as an entertainment lawyer with Frankfurt Kurnit Klein & Selz, a firm of twenty-four lawyers and fifty-seven employees.

Theater lawyers, Jean says, are really small-town practitioners. "They do a little bit of everything. They are involved in financing, licensing, and international copyright law." Per Jean, she and her colleagues work most closely with general managers of a production—essentially the chief operating officers. She has worked on hundreds of productions on Broadway, Off-Broadway, and the road including *Stomp, The Phantom of the Opera, Les Miserables,* and *Miss Saigon.*

She loves her association with theater.

Professor, Actor

Robyn Hunt; photograph courtesy of Kevin Clark

Robyn Hunt was singled out in 2008 as one of America's master teachers of acting by *American Theatre,* the magazine of the Theatre Communications Group. She is a recognized academic star, having taught, acted, presented, and lectured internationally.

As a member of Actors' Equity Association, she regularly acts in not-for-profit theaters around the country, usually playing important roles. For Connecticut Repertory Theatre she played the title role in Bertolt Brecht's *Mother Courage and Her Children.* For Actors Theatre of Louisville she acted Hesione in George Bernard Shaw's *Heartbreak House.* Looking back, Robyn estimates she has played more than fifty roles in the United States, Europe, and Japan.

This extraordinary acting/academic career had its beginnings in high school, where Robyn first thought of herself as a dancer. Her first experience was in La Jolla, California, when she was part of a featured chorus of tap dancers in Cole Porter's *Anything Goes.* Later she was Eliza Doolittle in *My Fair Lady,* and still later she took over the role of Nellie Forbush in Rodgers and Hammerstein's *South Pacific* on short notice. "How do you ever come down from those experiences?," she wonders today.

Robyn Hunt was hooked on theater. She loved rehearsal and performance. Robyn graduated with a B.A. from the University of California, San Diego. Then she earned a master of fine arts degree in acting from the same school. The question that faced her was how to make a living while still making social contributions to her community. She felt fulfilled, she notes, when exploring the issues of larger purpose raised by the academic community of an important university.

Her father had instilled in her the importance of making her own way in the world, and he told her not to be dependent on anyone for a living. Robyn realized that she came from a humble, middle-class background but didn't have the toughness and unbridled ambition to face a life of continuing auditions, so she sought a job aligned with theater, one that would allow her to teach and encourage future theater artists.

She became a teacher, first of undergraduates and then of graduate students in an M.F.A. program. Robyn earned tenure at the University of Washington in Seattle. During her eighteen years at Washington, she acted frequently around the country. These acting gigs "changed my teaching," Robyn said. She became even more attuned to what student actors needed to know and do; she brought back to her students what she learned from the process of acting professionally. Her department and university took note: she was given a distinguished teaching award

She has remained "aligned" with all aspects of theater. Robyn Hunt has published articles about acting. She has written plays, directed about twenty productions, and presented professional workshops and given lectures around the world.

She and her husband, the director/actor Steven Pearson, discovered that "a change of locale could, and probably *should* happen." Robyn began to realize that while Seattle was an "intellectually vibrant place to live," the gloomy weather was taking a toll on her disposition. They explored options and both accepted positions at the University of South Carolina in Columbia in 2006. She has earned her reputation as a nationally known professor who acts.

Actor, Opera Costume Head

Lesley C. Weston graduated from the drama division of the Juilliard School in New York. She gave up acting, however, when she was twenty-six. While going on auditions, she opened Ethel's Feathers, a vintage clothing store. That led to working with a Broadway costumer. Now she is costume-shop head for the Metropolitan Opera, a position she has held since 1985.

Her first job title at the Met, however, was "The Shopper." Lesley says, "that meant I did all the purchasing for all of the productions. Everything that had to do with the costumes." She maintains that "a costume is not clothing. It is not fashion. It is couture but not the kind of couture where one person wears an outfit three times. It's a combination of *soft* engineering and *soft* architectures." That means, she said, that the costume will last twenty-five or more years and withstand multiple alterations.

Lesley comes from a "sewing family." Her mother, she said, was "a couture-level seamstress, though not professionally. So was my grandmother." Her grandmother, she remembers, was the one who taught her how to embroider when she was four. Lesley is another actor who found her career in theater but not where she first thought.

Actor, Solo Playwright, Mother

Karen Eterovich planned to work in regional theaters after she trained as an actor. She was confident of this plan particularly because she did thirty-five plays in three years while earning an M.F.A. degree, including the one year she spent as

Karen Eterovic; photograph courtesy of Richard Kim

an intern at the Shakespeare Theatre in Washington, DC.

After graduating, Karen spent a year at Cornell University, acting there with the resident professional company. Later she acted for the Indiana Repertory Theatre. She had many high profile callbacks including ones for the Acting Company, Actors Theatre of Louisville, and the Public.

She did extra work in movies, but that did not lead to speaking parts. "It rarely does," she says. She recalled that Spike Lee was the "most humane" of the film directors she worked for, and she can be seen in his *Jungle Fever*. Acting work was sporadic, however, and it was difficult to make a living. A solution came to her—Karen decided to create a one-woman play for herself.

She knew how. As part of her acting training at the University of South Carolina, she was required to devise a one-person show; she built the production around the poetry of Sylvia Plath. That project was a success in an educational setting; in the real world she could not obtain the performance rights to the poems because Plath's estate refused.

Another subject leapt to mind. She had played a lead part, Angelica Bianca, in a play by Aphra Behn, *The Rover*, at Cornell. Behn (1640–1689), Karen discovered, was the first woman to earn her living by writing. There would be no copyright issues! Why not build a play around the life and times of Aphra Behn relying solely on Behn's words? "I wanted to use Aphra Behn's language to tell her story." The result is now *Love Arm'd: Aphra Behn and Her Pen*.

The sixty-minute play was an almost immediate success. Karen did not work through an agent or a booking agency. Instead she mailed cover letters and brochures to English departments, women's studies programs, and professors who specialized in seventeenth-century studies. Her first performance was at Wake Forest University. From there *Love Arm'd* took off. Karen has performed in 135 cities, many more than once.

After the Aphra Behn show was established, Karen devised a second show, around Jane Austen, *Cheer from Chawton*. The premise is that Austen is the mistress of ceremonies for a family version of *Pride and Prejudice* at Chawton Great House. Jane Austen festivals and theater and English departments book the show throughout the year. To her surprise, South Carolina Repertory Company, a regional theater on Hilton Head Island, booked her for performances in May 2011. She now publishes a newsletter, the *Aphra Jane News*, to announce her performances and post reviews and availability. The newsletter goes to former and prospective clients.

Karen is now married. She and her husband have a daughter. She is still acting; her husband, John, is supportive and wants her to continue performing.

Karen is an experienced classical actress who has worked for the Shakespeare Theatre (Washington, D.C.) and small companies, including Kings County Shakespeare and Blue Roses Productions. But when the acting jobs didn't materialize in sufficient number, she *made* the work. She's a member of Actors' Equity Association and Screen Actors Guild.

Actor, Playwright, Solo Performer

Mike Wiley; photography by Steve Exum

Like Karen Eterovich, Mike Wiley decided to write, promote, perform, and tour his own one-person shows. This choice was made after sporadic gigs touring in Shakespeare and children's theater companies. Unlike Karen's shows that feature a single character, Mike devised scripts with many characters, and he plays them all.

Mike Wiley's repertory now includes multi-character solo shows built around key events in African American history. They include plays about baseball player Jackie Robinson (*A Game Apart*), Martin Luther King (*Tired Souls: King and the Montgomery Bus Boycott*), and a slave's grandson who learned to read when he was ninety-eight years old (*Life Is So Good*). His very first script was about Henry "Box" Brown, a Virginia slave who mailed himself to Philadelphia and freedom (*One Nobel Journey*).

Wiley now has a repertory of eight plays that may be booked for schools and communities; he calls the productions "documentary theater." While performing these plays, he earned an M.F.A. acting degree from the University of North Carolina at Chapel Hill.

And, like Karen, Mike does not work through a booking agency. He learned about the business end of theater while touring with the children's theater company. Mike does it all himself, including booking, contracting, finding housing, and working with presenters. He also devised professional marketing materials along with a website, www.mikewileyproductions.com.

In short Mike Wiley is a working actor. His original plan was that, after earning an M.F.A., his solo work would earn him enough money to allow him time to audition for plays and films. But that was not the case. "Pretty soon, the solo work was all I was doing," he says. Yet he has appeared on national television.

Actor, Executive Director, Cabaret Artist

Sarah Boone; photograph by Laura Evans

Sarah Boone was a star student at Florida State University. She graduated magna cum laude with a B.A. in performance. Sarah spent about a decade pursuing an acting career after university before deciding to shift her focus. "As much as I enjoy performing," she says, "I really wanted to be able to have more input and control in the creative process. Producing began to hold more interest for me."

She made what she calls a "life change" when she entered the M.A. program in arts management at American University in Washington, D.C. After graduating with an interdisciplinary degree in arts management and communication, her career in theater management took off. Along the way Sarah spent time working as an administrator in important professional theaters, which included jobs as special projects manager at the Geffen Playhouse, an NFP theater in Los Angeles, and senior house manager at the Westside Theatre off-Broadway. She has also been a consulting producer with the California International Theatre Festival and, since 2000, has held the position of executive director at Theatre Jacksonville, a NFP community theater with a compelling history.

As executive director of Theatre Jacksonville, Sarah Boone found her "own artistic place." Her job, she notes, is really as a "producing artistic director," a combination of production coordinator and artistic overseer of all programs and services at the theater. She supervises three full-time employees—box office manager, technical director, and marketing/development officer. There are also three part-time positions—bookkeeper, education coordinator, and technical assistant. Sarah hires designers and directors on a per-show basis: "I have a group of artists upon whom I rely and use on a regular basis." "Theatre Jax" is a place where she can exercise her leadership skills while nurturing the artistic collaborations that occur under her watch. "Running the theater is very exciting and rewarding," she says, "but it also comes with its own stress. When goals are successfully met, that's great; but if there are problems, well, the buck still stops with me!"

With full- and part-time staff support, Theatre Jacksonville, founded in 1919, describes itself as "a volunteer based community theatre whose mission is to enrich lives and broaden cultural understanding through community participation in theatre arts." Each year more than four hundred volunteers share their time and talents as actors, crew members, ushers, and stage managers. Sarah has added, "And we really appreciate those audience members who 'volunteer' to buy tickets!"

Sarah also finds her "artistic place" performing in cabaret, an art form that has engaged her throughout her professional life. She recently debuted her show, "Sarah Boone: Songs at the Crossroads," at the prestigious Metropolitan Room in New York. She says she can't live without singing. "Whether it's on or off stage," she said, "I feel extremely privileged to make my living in theatre. The theatrical experience not only entertains us and enriches our lives; it promotes essential social dialogue that transforms us from singular beings to a community linked by deeper understanding. What an honor and joy to be part of that tradition." In short she's an actor and a manager.

Actor, Book Narrator

Ruth Ann Phimister; photograph courtesy of Michelle Hannay

Ruth Ann Phimister is an actress. "It's what I fall back on, the skill I have that sees me through." After thirty years in New York City, she relocated to the New England region of Actors' Equity Association in 2009. Ruth Ann's career has been a full one, mostly as a character actress. She's acted in regional theaters around the country, toured the United States and Canada in *Mornings at Seven,* narrated nearly one-hundred books for Recorded Books, LLC, and played off Broadway and off-off Broadway. She's acted for the Public Broadcasting System and done dinner theater.

She loves theater. "You're in a company of ten or fifteen, and in each company there are at least two 'keepers.' Actors move around a lot. But this is a business where you make extraordinary connections with special people. The keepers. The friends you'll keep up with no matter what."

Ruth Ann notes that not all friends and relatives will endorse a decision to become an actor. "During all my years as a professional actress and as a member of three theatrical unions, my mother came to only one show that I was in. My father, not one." So, she says, "you really have to say, 'I love this.' And mean it. You live an alternative life as an actor. You have to be prepared for your friends—and parents—to wonder when you're going to get 'a real job.'" Ruth Ann is an active member of Actors' Equity Association, Screen Actors Guild, and the American Federation of Television and Radio Artists.

After earning a master's degree in theater from the University of South Carolina, she returned to her native New York to try her hand at acting "when I was OLD!" She was thirty-three, armed with an undergraduate degree in philosophy from Drew University in New Jersey. "I really encourage those who want to act to get an undergraduate liberal arts degree. It stays with you," she said. She then earned another master's degree in library science and continued to study acting at HB Studio in New York.

Although formally trained as a research librarian, Ruth Ann worked as one only once full-time—with the Morgan Library for less than a year. She has been a part-timer, however, with the New-York Historical Society ("It was a fabulous job!") and the New York Public Library Theatre Collection. She remembers that it was through a library association conference in 1996 that she met the person who hired her as reader of fiction books for Recorded Books.

Her work as a narrator is extensive and rewarding, having read aloud books by such stellar authors as Jane Smiley, Anna Quindlen, and Tracy Chevalier. Her readings have twice won the prestigious Earphones Award given for, among other criteria, "narrative voice and style, vocal characterizations, and enhancement of the text."

Ruth Ann has also taught at times at the university level, at the American Academy of Dramatic Arts Evening School, and as a guest artist and substitute teacher in public and private schools in New York. Now Ruth Ann is proud to note she has made her modest living in the last decade solely as an actor. She remains an actor committed to acting.

Beyond the Facts

This random and unscientific series of profiles suggests many who want an acting career cannot support themselves by acting alone. This is not surprising; chapter 3 demonstrates that there are more aspiring actors that there are employment opportunities. Many of the people profiled here changed their career goals. Some discovered ways to incorporate acting with other related professions.

Beyond the facts lie opinions. Here are some of ours. People in all professions should be prepared to change their work, should their interests change or should adequate pay not be forthcoming. It is not a failure to change careers: it is the application of courage and common sense.

CHAPTER 8

Find Current Facts

Theater is always changing. Training opportunities alter over time. Job opportunities morph. Facts more up-to-date than a printed book can provide are available online and in periodicals. Theater training opportunities and job postings can be found in many places—in magazines and periodical books, on websites, and from theater organizations. At least six serial publications, most of which are likely to be found in a public or university library, reveal hundreds of current job and training opportunities. They provide even more facts about theater careers in every area of theater. Websites display a trove of job postings. No matter what the level of training already attained, these sources will prove useful for staying current in theater opportunities in work and training.

The periodicals, books, magazines, newspapers, and websites described here reiterate the story of this book: theater employment in the United States is not just for performers—singers, dancers, and actors. There are many opportunities for jobs backstage and in the offices of NFP theaters. These include positions as stage managers, designers, producers, business specialists, marketers, and many others. In short you can find current information for many of the positions described in chapter 1 by searching the sources identified in this discussion.

Periodicals

American Theatre

Published monthly by the Theatre Communications Group, a service organization for not-for-profit theaters, *American Theatre* focuses on the NFP theater universe. It concentrates its articles on theater artists—designers, actors, and playwrights—and often on production and administrative positions. Feature articles are mostly devoted to serious theater throughout the United States; not much about commercial theater will be found in its pages. *American Theatre* publishes new playscripts several times a year.

For the aspiring theater professional researching training opportunities, the basic value of *American Theatre* may very well be the advertisements placed by schools, both degree-granting and non-degree-granting programs. A recent issue of *American Theatre* contained ads for approximately thirty-two B.A. or B.F.A. programs, five M.A. programs, forty-three M.F.A. programs, five Ph.D. programs, and six nondegree programs. These ads gave important information about the specific nature of the training, faculty, and individual courses, as well as Internet URLs. This same issue identified dates and sites for unified admission auditions/ portfolio reviews by almost twenty training programs.

Dramatics

Published nine times a year, *Dramatics* is a theater magazine targeting high school theater students. In fact more than 80 percent of *Dramatics* readers are high school drama students. Published by the Educational Theatre Association, the parent organization of the International Thespian Society, the magazine features articles on new plays and also practical advice on developing skills in acting, directing, design, production, and other facets of theater. It also offers career-oriented profiles of working theater professionals. Two annual special issues focus on university theater programs (December) and summer theater work and study opportunities (February).

Back Stage

A tabloid format published weekly, *Back Stage* calls itself "The Actor's Resource." Feature material is included in each issue, but listings of job opportunities predominate. While *Back Stage* posts some opportunities for playwrights, stage managers, and other management positions, it primarily focuses on casting calls for auditions in New York and Los Angeles. The jobs may be outside of New York or Los Angeles, but the auditions are usually in those cities. In special issues in the spring, *Back Stage* lists training programs, some of which are provided by universities and some by acting coaches and the like.

The stated mission of *Back Stage* more fully describes the publication:

> *Back Stage* is proud to provide actors, actresses, models, singers, dancers, musicians, performers, staff, and crew with the best resources to enhance their careers, find open casting calls, and discover entertainment-industry jobs and auditions. *Back Stage* is also dedicated to providing casting directors, directors, producers, talent bookers, agents, employers, and managers with powerful tools to find great talent and to help manage casting calls, job notices, and multimedia resume submissions.

Back Stage is issued weekly and sells for $2.95 or $3.25 depending on the place of sale.

The following theater audition notices are typical of the information included in the postings:

Playmakers Repertory Company (Chapel Hill, NC) is casting *Angels in America*. The Pulitzer Prize–winning drama explores the first wave of the tsunami that became the AIDS epidemic set against the backdrop of the Reagan era. Joseph C. Haj, prod. artistic dir.; Brendon Fox, dir.; Tony Kushner, writer; Stephanie Klapper Casting, casting. Rehearsals begin Dec. 21; runs Jan. 29–March 6, 2011 in Chapel Hill, NC.

Seeking—Prior Walter, late 20s–early 30s, WASPy lover of Louis, emotionally open with others but is capable also of great wit and sassy, campy humor, passionate, self-deprecating, intense, huge emotional range. . . .

There follows a description of two other characters for which actors were being sought. While this production was seeking three actors, the play calls for eight. Clearly the company had actors in mind for the remaining five roles. The Playmakers casting call continued: "Auditions will be held by appt. only Oct. 18 in NYC. For consideration, send pix & resumes immediately to Stephanie Klapper Casting, 39 W. 19th St., 12th fl. NYC 1011. Mark on the outside of the envelope 'Angels in America—NYC Appointments—AEA member.' Note: Seeking submissions from Equity members only for these auditions. $700/wk (above minimum). Equity LORT D contract."

While the *Angels* audition was limited to union actors, *Back Stage* also lists opportunities for nonunion actors:

The Texas Shakespeare Festival is casting its 2011 season. Season includes: *Hamlet, The Taming of the Shrew, The Beaux Strategem,* and *Earnest in Love*. Ramond Caldwell, artistic dir. Contract runs May 21–August 9. Rehearses May 22–July 6; runs July 7–Aug 7, 2011 in Kilgore TX.

Seeking—Actors: 10 males and five female, to play all major roles; Interns: five males and two females. Note: Classical training and experience required; all must sing.

Also seeking staff—Technical Personnel.

Auditions will be held by appt. only Jan 14–17, 2011 in NYC and Jan 19–21 in L.A. Email pix & resumes to Auditions@TexasShakespeare.com or send to TSF, 1100 Broadway, Kilgore, TX 75662, Attn: Raymond Caldwell. Include your email address. Prepare two contrasting Shakespearean monologues (one in verse) and 16 bars of an appropriate song. If applying for a technical position, submit a cover letter, resume with email address, and two references. Deadline to submit is Nov 22, 2010. Pays $3,500 for major roles, plus travel provided; pays $1,250 for interns. Housing and 11 meals/wk. provided for all positions.

Live Design

Published nine times a year in a print edition, *Live Design* focuses on visual designers in all media—theater, commercials, clubs, concert and theater tours, theme parks, religious installations, corporate events, and trade shows. It is a creative and technical journal that covers lighting, staging, and projection subjects by reviewing the latest equipment developments and presenting photos of equipment in use. *Live Design* also presents "Broadway Master Classes" training sessions given by important designers of sound, projection, and lighting. In short this is a high-tech journal about cutting-edge visual and aural technology.

Through its online services (http://livedesignonline.com/), *Live Design* produces weekly updates ("Live Design Wire") and news and information on the newest technology advances ("Gear Wire: Sound, GW Projection, GW Lighting & Staging"). Often job opportunities are posted.

Variety

The premier source of entertainment news, *Variety* is the most widely recognized and respected U.S. weekly entertainment-trade magazine. Founded in 1905, *Variety* presents timely, credible, and straightforward news and analysis, information many believe is vital to their professions. It concentrates on all areas of show business, including theater. Those wishing to enter the profession should familiarize themselves with what plays and musicals are performing on Broadway and the road along with the box office receipts they garner. *Variety* often offers regional theater production reviews and descriptions of that are hard to find elsewhere.

The Dramatist

The Dramatist: The Journal of the Dramatists Guild of America is published every two months by the Dramatists Guild of America, the trade association for playwrights, theater composers, and lyricists. Contributors are usually people who have significant careers in the professional theater. While focused on playwriting, *The Dramatist* features articles on other aspects of theater. One recent issue, for example, had two articles devoted to producing with contributions by important commercial presenters and not-for-profit artistic directors. In another issue articles were focused on where theater professionals can find an artistic home. *The Dramatist* is a subscription magazine that can be found in some libraries.

Directory of Theatre Training Programs

About every two years, the *Directory of Theatre Training Programs* is published by Theatre Directories. The directory profiles admissions policies, tuition, faculty credentials, curriculum, facilities, productions, and philosophy of training at many programs, including those at universities with undergraduate and graduate degrees and at non-degree-granting schools. A recent issue had 475 listings. Many libraries will have copies in their reference areas.

University/Resident Theatre Association

U/RTA is a membership association that connects "graduate-level educational theater programs with professional theater and performing arts industries, promoting professional practices and artistic excellence in higher education." It assists students with their transition into the profession by organizing national unified auditions/portfolio reviews for its forty-three constituent members. These screenings invite actors, designers, directors, stage managers, and administrators who wish to pursue professional training at graduate programs. They are held annually in three locations, usually in New York, Chicago, and the Los Angeles area. U/RTA advertises these audition/portfolio reviews on its website (www.urta.com) and in *American Theatre.*

Web Listings
The Producer's Perspective

Ken Davenport, a Broadway and off-Broadway producer, has guided important (and not-so-important) plays to stages in New York and elsewhere. His Broadway producing credits include two David Mamet plays: *Oleanna,* starring Bill Pullman and Julia Stiles, and *Speed-the-Plow,* starring Raul Esparza. His production company was involved with Will Ferrell's *You're Welcome America; Blithe Spirit,* starring Angela Lansbury; and the musical *13.* Davenport's off-Broadway ventures include *Altar Boyz, The Awesome 80s Prom,* and *My First Time.* In short he is a working producer involved in the day-to-day business of putting on productions.

Davenport maintains a unique website, "The Producer's Perspective," that, in addition to Davenport's blog entries on theater, producing, and theater marketing, posts job opportunities (www.theproducersperspective.com). Picked at random, the following is an example of what might be found on line.

Audience Development and Marketing Manager—The Flea Theater
WHO: The Flea Theater
SEEKING: A Gangbuster Marketer to fill the role of Audience Development and Marketing Manager.
RESPONSIBILITIES: The Audience Development and Marketing Manager is The Flea's main contact with the general public and the primary focus is on the Flea's fast growing audience base. He or she oversees and deals with all marketing initiatives and materials, guerilla marketing, advertising, works with our press representative on the distribution of press materials, oversees the Flea web site and also oversees, coordinates and manages the "members

program." This position also manages, maintains and oversees the Flea database. This position will work with the Managing Director overseeing box office management. The Flea Theater uses Ovationtix as our ticketing and patron database.

REQUIREMENTS: Ideal candidate possesses an entrepreneurial spirit and two to three years experience in marketing, love for the theater, initiative, excellent organizational and communication skills, and the ability to multi-task in a fast-paced environment. Must be an independent decision maker with superior computer skills (including proficiency in Microsoft Word and Excel); experience with contact databases, theater ticketing software and graphic design programs (Quark, Photoshop) is also required. Graphic Design skills are a plus, as this position is responsible for all e-mail blasts (designed within Patron Mail).

WHEN: 10/25/2010

PAY: Salary is mid to upper 30s, based on experience. Medical benefits included.

HOW TO APPLY: Please email resume and two references to: Beth Dembros, Managing Director bethd@theflea.org.

Playbill

Playbill.com, another online site that lists job and training opportunities, sorts classified advertising under nine categories: academic, classes, design, directorial, editorial/writing, internship, other, performer, and technical. Playbill.com, the online subsidiary of the company that publishes theater programs around the country, claims: "Thousands of job seekers have found employment through our service, and you can, too!" What follows is a posting from the "other" category:

Front of House Usher

FOXWOODS THEATRE, the 13-year-old three-story Broadway Theatre complex and rehearsal studio in the heart of Times Square, seeks Full and Part Time FRONT OF HOUSE USHERS for the production "Spider-Man Turn Off the Dark." The Front of House Usher position will act as the theatre's ambassador, providing excellent customer service and ensuring public safety for all attending patrons.

Duties and responsibilities include: provide general information to patrons about the venue and production; properly scan tickets and direct & seat patrons to their ticketed seat; distribute show programs with stuffers; assist with rectifying patron's seating and ticketing issues; uphold and enforce the theatre's policies & procedures; knowledge and practice of emergency procedures; other duties as assigned by Theatre's management team.

Qualified candidates should have prior customer service experience, preferably in an entertainment venue with good interpersonal relations and communication skills.

Must possess a positive attitude, be flexible, friendly and courteous with patrons and fellow staff members and a team player.

Must be physically capable of performing all usher tasks including: able to stand for at least 3 hours; able to bend and lift up to 5 pounds; able to read small print; able to assist ADA patrons; able to be alert and think quickly in an emergency.

It is mandatory to join Union upon hire. Send cover letter and resume to House Manager, Foxwoods Theatre at theatremanagementgroup@gmail.com. Please put Usher in Subject line of email. No phone calls please.

Theatre Development Fund

"PxP," published quarterly by the Theatre Development Fund (TDF), describes itself as "the theater magazine by and for teens." Hardcopy printings can be found in some locations around the Broadway theater district and an Acrobat version is available at the TDF website (www.tdf.org). TDF is a not-for-profit group that runs educational programs and operates TKTS ticket booths in three New York City locations that offer same-day tickets at a discount, usually 50 percent. Commercial and NFP theaters, as well as dance and opera companies, which have not sold out for a performance, may release tickets to TKTS for discounted sale. TDF also operates a membership program for full-time students, teachers, union members, retirees, civil service employees, staff members of not-for-profit organizations, performing arts professionals, and members of the armed forces or clergy at a fee of thirty dollars per year; members can log-in and, if tickets are available, they can be ordered, usually at a 60 percent discount.

Beyond the Facts

The printed and online resources detailed in this chapter can help the beginning theatre enthusiast keep current in what's happening in theater, including graduate training programs and employment opportunities. Clearly these sources are not exhaustive. Explore!

Beyond the facts lie opinions. Here are some of ours. Keep current. Know what's happening in the field of theatre. Develop an understanding of professional theater beyond the information presented here. *Theatre Careers* is a beginning; it is not "all you need to know to work in theater."

Afterword

Love Theater without a Career in Theater

Theater Careers was introduced with the premise that some people catch the theater bug. From early experiences in school or community theater, these folks find an activity—and a tribe of like-minded people—that excites them and motivates them to want more. We know because many years ago we fell under the spell of theater too.

But pursuing a career in theater is a risky plan. All careers are risky to varied extents, with surprises and reversals, but theater is a particularly challenging career choice. Anyone who says otherwise is ignoring the facts. The facts are

There are more kinds of jobs in professional theater than most people imagine; acting isn't the only choice.

Theater education can take many paths and to choose among them, the end goal should be considered carefully or time and money will be squandered.

Someone with a B.A. in dramatic arts makes less on average than the average holder of a B.A. does, and is more likely to work part-time; still, drama B.A. degree holders in the workforce report about the same satisfaction with their jobs, on average, as do all B.A. holders in the workforce.

Averages hide much variation; thus there are theater graduates doing "well" to "very well" financially in the workforce.

Theater jobs are everywhere but are largely focused in bigger cities, the extreme case being the concentration of jobs in New York City.

Unions make rules, but they don't make jobs; in some cities, union membership may limit job choice.

A career isn't chosen only once, never to be changed; in fact most people change careers at least once during their working lives.

If the facts about a theater career are daunting or discouraging, there are ways to continue to be involved with theater *without having a career in theater*. Some of the suggestions we make are obvious; some may be surprising.

Be in the Audience

Attend theater whenever you can, in your own community and elsewhere. Theater needs audiences as much as it needs artists, administrators, and technicians.

Read

Stay current with theater by reading newspapers and journals. Some very good feature writing and reviews on theater are available on the Internet at no cost as of this writing, including what is found in the *New York Times* and the *Washington Post* . The weekly entertainment trade publication *Variety* is not free on the Internet at this time, but *Variety* offers more reviews and information about London and regional U.S. theater than are available anywhere else. Many libraries subscribe to all three of these publications.

Become an individual member of the Theatre Communications Group and, by doing so, get a subscription to its monthly full-color journal, *American Theatre*.

Read plays. Few plays now are published in trade-book form so libraries generally don't stock plays. *American Theatre* reprints in total about four scripts a year. If all else fails, the staff at the Drama Book Shop can help you find a script. The physical store is located in midtown Manhattan on 40th St between 7th and 8th avenues. The Internet store is http://www.dramabookshop.com/.

Professionals and Consultants

Not-for-profit theaters need professionals and consultants, such as lawyers, certified public accountants, human resources professionals, and the like. Larger NFPs will pay for these services; smaller ones may welcome *pro bono* work. You can be a lawyer, making your parents proud, and still keep a toe in the theater world. (By the way, lawyers sometimes study acting because trial lawyers "perform" for a judge and jury.)

Volunteer

Although large NFP theaters will be highly professionalized, most still welcome volunteers. Be an usher and really learn about theater by seeing the same production several times. Staff the gift shop. Stuff envelopes. Ask how you can help.

The amateur community theater will welcome volunteers in a wider array of work, perhaps even directing, designing, crewing, performing, and elsewhere.

In communities with a free weekly newspaper, volunteers may be accepted to write reviews of local theater.

Donate and/or Invest

If you can, donate money to a NFP theater whose work has meaning for you. Or you might invest in a commercial production. Know that because commercial theater is highly risky, an investor should be prepared to lose the entire investment. In fact, because of the level of risk, the U.S. Securities and Exchange Commission requires investors in commercial theater to be "qualified purchasers," which means to be eligible, for example, to invest ten thousand dollars in a commercial production, an investor must have a net value in excess of $1 million, not counting a primary residence.

See Theater When Traveling

It can be very exciting to see theater in new cities. After a day of sightseeing or of business meetings, an evening in the theater can be a particularly welcome change, relaxing and invigorating.

Theater needs artists, technicians, stagehands, and ushers. It also needs investors, donors, and especially audience members. Indulge your love of theater no matter how you make your living.

The American Community Survey

Selected Results of the American Community Survey and the US Census

	1990 Census	2000 Census	Growth	2005 ACS	Growth
Actor	35,916	38,605	7.5%	41,742	8.1%
Dancer and Choreographer	21,771	26,915	23.6%	29,667	10.2%
Designers	619,328	749,335	21.0%	802,927	7.2%
Producers and Directors	120,609	139,335	15.5%	140,044	0.5%
Writers and Authors	133,471	162,155	21.5%	188,555	16.3%
Total Civilian Labor Force	123,473,450	137,668,735	11.5%	146,559,784	6.5%

According to a US Census survey, the number of most jobs filled in artistic areas that include theater increased between 2000 and 2005 at a rate higher than the increase in the total labor force. The exception is jobs for producers and directors; these barely increased at all.

Selected Median Income from the American Community Survey

	Median Income for all workers	Median Income for full-year, full-time workers only
Civilian Labor Force	$30,100	$38,700
Actors	$23,400	$31,500
Dancers, choreographers	$20,000	$34,600
Designers	$34,400	$42,000
Producers and directors	$47,100	$52,500
Writers and authors	$38,800	$50,800

Shown here are the median income from wages for people employed less than full-year, full-time and those working full-year, full-time. For those theater professionals finding full-year, full-time work, average wages are higher in every job classification.

The National Science Foundation's
"National Survey of College Graduates"

The National Science Foundation (NSF), through the US Census Bureau, conducts regular, large surveys of career outcomes for university graduates, called the "National Survey of College Graduates." Although the NSF is interested in job outcomes for holders of degrees in science and engineering, its data set is accessible to anyone to answer research questions outside scientific fields. The numbers of survey respondents with a B.A. in dramatic arts, weighted for the whole population, according to the NSF estimates, puts current holders of dramatic arts BAs nationwide at 234,702, as of the week including October 1, 2003. To give this figure perspective, the NSF survey estimates the number of all US degree holders at 50.3 million. Less than one-half percent of degree holders in the United States hold a major in dramatic arts.

Some Measures from Selected Undergraduate Majors

			Bachelor Degree Major	
	All Respondents	*Dramatic Arts*	*English*	*Business*
Average salary	$68,455	$46,415	$44,677	$62,853
Percentage of jobs that are				
Full-time	89.8%	80.3%	83.8%	92.3%
Part-time	10.2%	19.7%	16.7%	7.7%
Percentage of jobs related to degree				
Closely	61.4%	50.0%	57.5%	42.1%
Somewhat	23.3%	20.6%	20.5%	40.0%
Not at all	15.3%	29.4%	22.0%	17.9%
Percentage who are satisfied with job				
Very satisfied	46.3%	42.3%	46.5%	45.1%
Somewhat satisfied	44.3%	47.2%	43.0%	45.2%
Somewhat dissatisfied	7.4%	8.5%	8.0%	7.4%
Very dissatisfied	2.0%	2.0%	2.4%	2.3%
Percentage by gender satisfied				
Female	43.0%	62.8%	65.3%	35.8%
Male	57.0%	37.2%	34.7%	64.2%

This table contains selected statistics calculated by the authors from the raw data sets of the National Survey of College Graduates, October 2003. Holders of dramatic arts or English degrees earn less than the average college graduates, but are not less satisfied with their jobs. Gender may play a part in the salary differences, since many more females than males in this survey held dramatic arts or English degrees. Females are on average paid less than men in all professions.

AAE	Amusement Area Employees
ADG	Art Directors Guild
AE	Arena Employees
AFE	Arena Facility Employees
AG&AOE&GA	Animation Guild and Affiliated Optical Electronic and Graphic Arts
AMPE	Airline Motion Picture Employees
AMTS	Admissions, Mutual Ticket Sellers
APC	Affiliated Property Craftspersons
ATPAM	Association of Theatrical Press Agents and Managers
BPTS	Ball Park Ticket Sellers
C	Camerapersons
CDG	Costume Designers Guild
CHE	Casino Hotel Employees
E,S&CST	Electronic, Sound & Computer Service Technicians
EE	Exhibition Employees
EE/BPBD	Exhibition Employees/Bill Posters, Billers and Distributors
FAE	First Aid Employees
ICG	International Cinematographers Guild
LF/VT	Laboratory Film/Video Technicians
M	Mixed
MAHS	Make-Up Artists & Hair Stylists
MAHSG	Make-Up Artists & Hair Stylists Guild
MPC	Motion Picture Costumers
MPEG	Motion Picture Editors Guild (inclusive of Editors and Story Analysts)
MPP,AVE&CT	Motion Picture Projectionists, Audio Visual Engineers and Computer Technicians
MPP,O&VT	Motion Picture Projectionists, Operators and Video Technicians
MPP,O,VT&AC	Motion Picture Projectionists, Operators, Video Technicians & Allied Crafts
MPP,O,VT&CT	Motion Picture Projectionists, Operators, Video Technicians & Computer Technicians

MPP,VT&CT	Motion Picture Projectionists, Video and Computer Technicians
MPSELT	Motion Picture Studio Electrical Lighting Technicians
MPSG/CS	Motion Picture Studio Grips/Crafts Service
MPSP&SW	Motion Picture Set Painters & Sign Writers
MPSPT	Motion Picture Studio Production Technicians
MPST	Motion Picture Studio Teachers and Welfare Workers
MPVT/LT/AC&GE	Motion Picture Videotape/Laboratory Technicians/Allied Crafts and Government Employees
MT	Mail Telephone Order Clerks
O	Operators
PC,CP&HO	Production Coordinators, Craftservice Providers & Honeywagon Operators
PST,TE,VAT&SP	Production Sound Technicians, Television Engineers, Video Assist Technicians and Studio Projectionists
S	Stage Employees
S&FMT	Sound & Figure Maintenance Technicians
SA&P	Scenic Artists and Propmakers
SM	Studio Mechanics
SM&BT	Studio Mechanics & Broadcast Technicians
SS,CC,A&APSG	Script Supervisors, Continuity Coordinators, Accountants and Allied Production Specialists Guild
SS,PC,CC&PA	Script Supervisors, Production Coordinators, Continuity Coordinators & Production Accountants
T	Theatre Employees - Special Departments
T&T	Treasurers & Ticket Sellers
TBR&SE	Television Broadcasting Remote & Studio Employees
TBSE	Television Broadcasting Studio Employees
TSA	Ticket Sales Agents
TW,MAHS	Theatrical Wardrobe, Make-up Artists and Hair Stylists
TWU	Theatrical Wardrobe Union
USA	United Scenic Artists

IATSE Stage Employee Locals

Local Number	*Jurisdiction*
1	New York–Westchester–Putnam Counties, N.Y.
2	Chicago, Ill.
3	Pittsburgh–New Castle, Pa.
4	Brooklyn–Queens, N.Y.
5	Cincinnati–Hamilton–Fairfield–Springdale–Oxford, Ohio
6	St. Louis, Mo.
7	Denver–Boulder, Colo.
8	Philadelphia, Pa./Camden–Mercer County, N.J.
9	Syracuse, N.Y.
10	Buffalo, N.Y.
11	Boston, Mass.
12	Columbus–Newark–Marysville–Delaware, Ohio
13	Minneapolis–St. Cloud–Little Falls–Brainerd–St. John's Univ.–Coll. of St. Benedict–St. Paul, Minn.
14	Albany–Schenectady–Amsterdam, N.Y.
15	Seattle–Everett–Olympia–Tacoma–Bremerton–Bellingham–Anacortes–Mt. Vernon–Sedro Wooley–Port Angeles–Burlington–Concrete–Stanwood–Marysville–Snohomish–Monroe–Longview, Wash.
16	San Francisco–Marin City–Santa Rosa–Lake Mendocino–Sonoma–Napa City–San Mateo Cty, Calif.
17	Louisville–Frankfort–Danville, Ky.
18	Milwaukee–Waukesha, Wis.
19	Baltimore, Md.
21	Newark–Middlesex–Mercer–Ocean and Union Counties–Asbury Park–Long Beach, N.J.
22	Washington, D.C./Washington D.C. Suburbs, Md./Northern Va.
24	Toledo–Lima–Marion–Bowling Green–Tiffin–Findlay, Ohio
25	Rochester, N.Y.
27	Cleveland–Sandusky–Erie County, Ohio
30	Indianapolis–Kokomo–Richmond–Earlham College–Logansport–Peru–Wabash–Connersville–Muncie–Portland–Anderson, Ind.

Local Number	*Jurisdiction*
31	Kansas City–St. Joseph, Mo./Kansas City–Topeka–Lawrence–Emporia, Kans.
32	Duluth, Minn.
33	Loangeles–Long Beach–Pasadena–Santa Monica, Calif.
38	Detroit–Pontiac–Mt. Clemens–Port Huron, Mich.
39	New Orleans, La.
42	Omaha–Fremont, Ne./Council Bluffs–Sioux City, Iowa
46	Nashville, Tenn.
47	Pueblo, Colo.
48	Akron–Canton–Mansfield, Ohio
49	Terre Haute, Ind.
50	Sacramento–Chico–Stockton–Marysville, Calif.
51	Houston–Galveston, Tex.
53	Springfield–Pittsfield, Mass.
54	Binghamton, N.Y.
56	Montreal, Quebec, Canada
58	Toronto, Ontario, Canada
59	Hudson County, N.J.
66	Dayton–Darke–Miami–Champaign Counties, Ohio
67	Des Moines–Ames–Waukee–Mason City, Iowa
69	Memphis, Tenn.
74	Southern Connecticut
76	San Antonio, Tex.
78	Birmingham, Ala.
82	Wilkes-Barre, Pa.
84	Hartford–New London–northern Connecticut
85	Davenport, Iowa/Moline–Rock Island, Ill.
87	Richmond–Petersburg–Charlottesville, Va.
97	Reading, Pa.
98	Harrisburg–Hershey–Carlisle, Pa.
99	State of Utah/Boise–Nampa–Caldwell–Twin Falls–Sun Valley, Idaho
101	Youngstown–Niles–Warren, Ohio
102	Evansville, Ind.
107	Alameda Cty–Oakland–Berkley–Contra Costa Cty–Solano Cty–Richmond–Concord, Calif.
112	Oklahoma City, Okla.
113	Erie, Pa.
114	Portland–Lewiston–Augusta–Bangor, Maine
118	Vancouver, B.C., Canada

Local Number	Jurisdiction
122	San Diego, Calif.
124	Joliet, Ill.
126	Ft. Worth–Arlington–Denton–Gainesville–Grapevine, Tex.
127	Dallas–Grand Prairie–McKinney, Tex.
129	Hamilton–Brantford, Ontario, Canada
138	Springfield–Jacksonville, Ill.
140	Chattanooga, Tenn.
142	Mobile, Ala.
146	Ft. Wayne, Ind.
158	Fresno–Modesto–Stockton, Calif.
168	Vancouver Island B.C., Canada
197	Knoxville–Maryville–Alcoa–Gatlinburg, Tenn.
200	Allentown–Easton, Pa.
201	Flint–Owosso, Mich.
210	Edmonton, Alberta, Canada
212	Calgary, Alberta, Canada
220	Sioux Falls–Mitchell–Huron, S. Dak.
229	Ft. Collins, Colo./Cheyenne–Laramie, Wyo.
271	Charleston, W. Va.
284	Wilmington, Del.
285	Norfolk–Chesapeake–Portsmouth–Virginia Beach, Va.
298	Shreveport, La.
336	Phoenix–Prescott, Ariz.
340	Nassau/Suffolk Counties of Long Island, N.Y.
354	Tulsa–Ponca City, Okla.
471	Ottawa–Kingston–Belleville, Ontario, Canada
614	San Bernardino–Riverside–Pomona–Redlands–Ontario–Claremont–Barstow–Bishop–Lancaster–Victorville, Calif.
629	Augusta, Ga.
647	Naples–Fort Myers–Marco Island, Fla.
918	Anchorage, Alaska
919	Burlington, Vt./Hanover–Lebanon, N.H.
927	Atlanta, Ga.

Abarbanel, Jonathan. "Sweet Home Chicago: Actors Find Life Is Sweet on Windy City Stages," *Back Stage East*, August 16, 2007, 26–29.

Actor's Equity. "About Equity." http://www.actorsequity.org/docs/about/aboutequity_Web.pdf. Accessed April 25, 2011.

American Association of University Professors. "No Refuge: The Annual Report on the Economic Status of the Profession, 2009–2010." http://www.aaup.org/NR/rdonlyres/AFB34202–2D42–48B6–9C3B-52EC3D86F605/0/zreport.pdf. Accessed April 25, 2011.

American Theatre, July/August 2011 (source of marketing slogans in text).

"America's Best Colleges." *U.S. News and World Report* 146 (September 2009): 75–98.

Andrews, Starra. *The Pursuit of Acting: Working Actors Share Their Experience and Advice*, Westport, Conn.: Praeger, 1998.

"Are Too Many Students Going to College?" Chronicle Review section, *Chronicle of Higher Education*, November 8, 2009. http://chronicle.com/article/Are-Too-Many-Students-Going/49039/. Accessed June 20, 2011.

Arum, Richard, and Losipa Roksa. *Academically Adrift: Limited Learning on College Campuses*. Chicago: University of Chicago Press, 2011.

Association of Theatrical Press Agents and Managers. "Minimum Basic Agreement between ATPAM and the League of Off-Broadway Theatres and Producers," July 1, 2001, through June 30, 2006. http://www.offbroadway.org/ OB_MBA_2001a.pdf. Accessed April 25, 2011.

Bofshever, Michael. *Your Face Looks Familiar . . . : How to Get Ahead as a Working Actor*, Portsmouth, N.H.: Heinemann, 2006.

Cairns, Adrian. *The Making of the Professional Actor*. London: Peter Owen, 1996.

Carey, Nancy, Brian Kleiner, Rebecca Porch, and Elizabeth Farris. "Arts Education in Public Elementary and Secondary Schools: 1999–2000." National Center For Education Statistics, June 2002. http://nces.ed.gov/pubsearch/pubsinfo.asp?pubid=2002131. Accessed October 29, 2011.

Center on Education and the Work Force. http://cew.georgetown.edu/. Accessed April 25, 2011.

Chambers and Partners website. http://www.chambersandpartners.com/.

Charles, J. *Directory of Theatre Training Programs: Profiles of College and Conservatory Programs Throughout the United States*, 8th edition. Dorset, Vt.: Theatre Directories, 2006.

Cohen, Robert, and James Calleri. *Acting Professionally: Raw Facts about Careers in Acting*, 7th ed. New York: Palgrave Macmillan, 2009.

College Board Advocacy & Policy Center. http://advocacy.collegeboard.org. Accessed April 25, 2011.

Conn, Peter. "We Need to Acknowledge the Realities of Employment in the Humanities." Chronicle Review section, *Chronicle of Higher Education,* April 4, 2010. http://chronicle.com/article/Forum-The-Need-for-Reform-in/64887/.

Coppens, Julia York. "Choices." *Dramatics* 71 (December 2000): 6–9.

Deresiewicz, William. "Faulty Towers: The Crisis in Higher Education." *Nation,* May 4, 2011 http://www.thenation.com/article/160410/faulty-towers-crisis-higher-education. Accessed May 7, 2011.

Diamond, David, and Terry Berliner, eds. *Stage Directors Handbook: Opportunities for Directors and Choreographers.* New York: Theatre Communications Group, 1998.

DiPaola, Steven. "2008–2009 Seasonal Report." Actors Equity. http://www.actorsequity.org/docs/about/AEA_Annual_2008.pdf. Accessed February 2011.

———. "2009–2010 Seasonal Report." Actors Equity. http://www.actorsequity.org/docs/about/AEA_Annual_2009.pdf. Accessed August 2011.

Donahue, Tim, and Jim Patterson. *Stage Money: The Business of the Professional Theater.* Columbia: University of South Carolina Press, 2010.

Dramatics. http://schooltheatre.org/publications/dramatics. Accessed April 25, 2011.

Dramatists Guild. http://www.dramatistsguild.com/

Engelman, Liz. "Employment Guidelines (Adopted by Literary Managers and Dramaturgs of the Americas, November 2000) Abridged/Edited Draft [2002]." http://old.lmda.org/blog/_archives/2005/1/11/237625.html. Accessed April 25, 2011.

Everett, Carole J. *College Guide for Performing Arts Majors.* Lawrenceville, N.J.: Peterson's, 2006.

Feldman, Adam. "Q & A: Tony Kushner." *Time Out New York,* May 23, 2011. http://newyork.timeout.com/arts-culture/theater/1451999/qa-tony-kushnerj. Accessed June 3, 2011.

Field, Shelly. *Career Opportunities in Theatre and the Performing Arts.* New York: Ferguson, 2006.

Flanagan, Markus. *One Less Bitter Actor: The Actor's Survival Guide.* Boulder, Colo.: Sentient Publications, 2008.

Fogg, Neeta P., Paul E. Harrington, and Thomas F. Harrington. *College Majors Handbook with Real Career Paths and Payoffs,* 2nd ed. Indianapolis, Ind.: JIST Publishing, 2004.

Foundation Center. http://foundationcenter.org /findfunders/990finder/. Accessed April 25, 2011.

Gaquin, Deidre. *Artists in the Workforce: 1990–2005.* Washington, D.C.: National Endowment for the Arts, May 2008.

Gillespie, Bonnie. *Self-Management for Actors: Getting Down to (Show) Business.* Los Angeles: Cricket Feet Publishing, 2003.

Godofsky, Jessica, Cliff Zukin, and Carl Van Horn. "Unfulfilled Expectations: Recent College Graduates Struggle in a Troubled Economy." *Worktrends,* Rutgers University, May 2011 http://news.rutgers.edu/medrel/news-releases/2011/05/unfulfilled-expectat-20110523. Accessed June 20, 2011.

Goldberg, Jan. *Great Jobs for Theater Majors.* New York: McGraw-Hill, 2005.

Grady, Jamie. *Actors, Inc.: How to Get the Next Gig—and Still Pay Your Rent.* Portsmouth, N.H.: Heinemann, 2007.

Harvard College. "Academic Requirements." http://www.college.harvard.edu/icb/icb. do?keyword=k61161&pageid=icb.page284442. Accessed April 25, 2011.

Harvard University. "Tuition at Harvard Schools: FY1990 – FY2010." http://www .provost.harvard.edu/institutional_research/Provost_-_FB2009_10_Sec03_Tuition. pdf. Accessed April 25, 2011.

Hoffer, Thomas B., and Vincent Welch, Jr. "Time to Degree of U.S. Research Doctorate Recipients." National Science Foundation, March 2006. http://www.nsf.gov/statistics/ infbrief/nsf06312/. Accessed April 25, 2011.

Horwitch, Lauren. "The Union Label: Whether, When, and How to Join a Guild." *Back Stage East,* July 19, 2007. http://find.galegroup.com.pallas2.tcl.sc.edu/gtx/retrieve .do?contentSet=IAC-Documents&resultListType=RESULT_LIST&qrySerId=Locale %28en%2C%2C%29%3AFQE%3D%28ti%2CNone%2C15%29the+union+label %24&sgHitCountType=None&inPS=true&sort=DateDescend&searchType=Ad vancedSearchForm&tabID=T003&prodId=ITOF&searchId=R1&currentPosition=9 &userGroupName=usclibs&docId=A166824464&docType=IAC. Subscription site. Accessed June 20, 2010.

Horwitz, Simi. "All Roads Lead to the General Manager," *Back Stage,* June 30, 2005. http:// www.allbusiness.com/services/amusement-recreation-services/4587049–1.html. Accessed April 25, 2011.

Innovative Theatre Foundation. "Demographic Study of Off-Off-Broadway Practitioners." Innovative Theatre Foundation, 2010. http://www.nyitawards.com/survey/oob demographics.pdf. Accessed October 29, 2011.

International Association of Theatrical Stage Employees, Local 1 website. http://www .iatselocalone.org.

International Association of Theatrical Stage Employees, Local 18032 website. http:// www.unionworkers.com/local_union/iatse/iatse_local_18032.php. Accessed April 25, 2011.

International Association of Theatrical Stage Employees, Local 306 website. http://www .local306.org/. Accessed April 25, 2011.

International Association of Theatrical Stage Employees, Local 751 website. http:// local751.com/GeneralInfo/Generalhome.htm. Accessed April 25, 2011.

Jay, Annie, with LuAnne Fei. *Stars in Your Eyes . . . Feet on the Ground.* Dorset, Vt.: Theatre Directories, 1999.

Jeffri, Joan, Robert Greenblatt, and Catherine Sessions. "The Artists Training and Career Project: Actors." Report prepared for the Research Center for Arts and Culture, Columbia University, 1992. http://www.tc.columbia.edu/centers/rcac/pdf/FullReport _31.pdf. Accessed October 29, 2011.

Jeffri, Joan. *The Actor Speaks: Actors Discuss their Experiences and Careers.* Westport, CT: Greenwood Press, 1994.

Kellogg, Marjorie Bradley. "Design and the Bottom Line: For designers, it's harder than ever to make ends meet." *American Theatre* 18 (November 2001): 34–39.

Lawler, Mike. *Careers in Technical Theater.* New York: Allworth Press, 2007.

League of Resident Theatres website. http://www.lort.org/

Leonhardt, David. "At Colleges, Too Few Diplomas." *New York Times*, September 9, 2009, B1, B5.

———. "Colleges Are Failing in Graduation Rates." *New York Times*, September 9, 2009. http://www.nytimes.com/2009/09/09/business/economy/09leonhardt.html?scp=1&sq=colleges%20are%20failing%20in%20graduation%20rates&st=cse

———. "Even for Cashiers, College Pays Off." *New York Times*, June 26, 2011, SR 3.

———. "In Wreckage of Lost Jobs, Lost Power." *New York Times*, January 19, 2011, Page B1.

———. "The College Calculation: How Much Does Higher Education Matter?" *New York Times Sunday Magazine*, September 27, 2009, 13–16.

———. "The True Price of Admission." *New York Times*, November 22, 2009, 10.

Leptak-Moreau, Jeffrey. "Where Are You Going?" *Dramatics* 76 (December 2005): 6–13.

Lewin, Tamar. "What's the Most Expensive College? The Least? Education Dept. Puts It All Online." *New York Times*, June 30, 2011, http://www.nytimes.com/2011/06/30/education/30collegeweb.htm, accessed June 30, 2011.

Live Design Magazine website. http://livedesignonline.com/.

London, Todd and Ben Pesner. *Outrageous Fortune, the Life and Times of the New American Play.* New York: Theatre Development Fund, 2009.

Loveland, Elaina. *Creative Colleges: A Guide for Student Actors, Artists, Dancers, Musicians and Writers.* Belmont, CA: SuperCollege, LLC, 2008.

Marklein, Mary Beth. "College Graduates Break even by Age 33." *USA Today,* September 21, 2010.

Marks, Peter. "Young Md. Actor Sails to Broadway's 'Brighton Beach.'" *Washington Post,* October 18, 2009. http://www.washingtonpost.com/wp-dyn/content/article/2009/10/17/AR2009101701970_2.html. Accessed April 25, 2011.

Mauro, Lucia. *Careers for the Stage-Struck and Other Dramatic Types.* Chicago: VGM Career Books, 2004.

Mayleas, Ruth. *Theatre Artist's Resources.* New York: Watson-Guptill, Publications, 1999.

McGrath, Charles. "A Return to Southie by Way of Broadway." *New York Times,* February 6, 2011, Arts & Leisure, 6.

Menand, Louis. "Live and Learn: Why We Have College." *New Yorker*, June 6, 2011, 74–79.

———. *The Marketplace of Ideas.* New York: W.W. Norton & Co., 2010.

Miller, Ben, and Phuong Ly. "College Dropout Factories." *Washington Monthly*, August 23, 2010, http://www.washingtonmonthly.com/college_guide/ feature/college_dropout_factories.php. Accessed August 24, 2010.

Moody, James L., ASLD [American Society of Lighting Directors]. *The Business of Theatrical Design.* New York: Allworth Press, 2002.

Moore, Dick. *Opportunities in Acting Careers.* New York: McGraw-Hill, 2005.

Moore, John. "Theater: Only a Few Make Living from Stage Alone." *Denver Post*, July 14, 2008. http://www.denverpost.com/ci_9843952. Accessed June 20, 2011.

"The Myth of the Starving Artist." *Inside Higher Ed*, May 6, 2011. http://www.inside highered.com/news/2011/05/03/graduates_of_arts_programs_fare_better_in_job _market_than_assumed. Accessed June 20, 2011.

National Association of Schools of Art and Design. "Advisory Regarding Credit Hour Requirements for the Master of Fine Arts Degree in Theatre." http://nast.arts-accredit .org/site/docs/NAST%20MFA%20Policies/NAST%20Advisory%20on%20Credit% 20Hour%20Requirements%20for%20the%20MFA.pdf. Accessed April 25, 2011.

National Association of Schools of Theatre website. http://nast.arts-accredit.org/. Accessed April 25, 2011.

National Center for Educational Statistics, U.S. Department of Education. *Digest of Education Statistics 2008* (March 2009).

National Conservatory of Dramatic Arts. "Actor Training Programs." http://www .theconservatory.org/TrainingPrograms.html. Accessed April 25, 2011.

National Office for Arts Accreditation website. http://www.arts-accredit.org/. Accessed April 25, 2011.

National Science Foundation. "National Survey of College Graduates." http://www.nsf .gov/statistics/srvygrads/. Accessed February 2011.

Neighborhood Playhouse School of Theatre website. http://www.neighborhoodplay house.org/. Accessed April 25, 2011.

"New York Acting Schools and Coaches." *Back Stage*, April 13, 2011. http://www.back stage.com/bso/production-listings/new-york-acting-schools-coaches-1005014702 .story. Accessed June 21, 2011.

Novick, Rebecca. "Rising to the Middle." *Bay Area Theatre*. http://theatreba.kattare.com/ mag/article.jsp?thispage=archives.jsp&id=613&hi=1&css=1. Accessed May 27, 2011.

Ohio University School of Theatre catalog, undated. http://www.catalogs.ohio.edu/ preview_entity.php?catoid=16&ent_oid=1049&returnto=79. Accessed April 25, 2011.

Oxman, Steve. "New Works Storm Windy City: Prolific Theater Scene Benefits Local Coin, Eager Auds." *Variety*, February 7–13, 2011, 48.

Pappano, Laura. "The Master's as the New Bachelor's." *New York Times*, July 22, 2011, Education, Life Supplement, 1.

Patterson, Jim, Donna McKenna-Crook, and Melissa Swick Ellington. *Theatre in the Secondary School Classroom: Methods & Strategies for the Beginning Teacher*. Portsmouth, N.H.: Heinemann, 2006.

PCPA Theaterfest. "PCPA 2 Year Acting Conservatory." http://www.pcpa.org/conservatory/ actingjourney.html. Accessed April 25, 2011.

Pérez-Peña, Richard and Daniel E. Slotnick. "Gaming the College Rankings." *New York Times*, February 1, 2012, A14.

Perry, Richard. "New York Stagecraft Plies the High Seas." *New York Times*, March 13, 2012, Arts, 1.

Piepenburg, Erik. "It's All about Holding Hands and Stitching Hems." *New York Times*, June 25, 2011, C1, C5.

Planty, Michael, William Hussar, Thomas Snyder, Grace Kena, Angelina KewalRamani, Jana Kemp, Kevin Bianco, and Rachel Dinkes. *The Condition of Education 2009*.

National Center for Education Statistics. http://nces.ed.gov/programs/coe/2009/pdf/
   40_2009.pdf. Accessed April 25, 2011.

Professor X. *In the Basement of the Ivory Tower: Confessions of an Accidental Academic.*
   New York: Viking, 2011.

Public Agenda. "Can I Get a Little Advice Here?" [2010]. http://www.publicagenda.org/
   theirwholelivesaheadofthem?qt_active=1. Accessed April 25, 2011.

Rand, Ronald, and Luigi Scorcia. *Acting Teachers of America: A Vital Tradition.* New York:
   Allworth Press, 2007.

Raymond, Gerard. "Training to Stand Out: Casting Directors Reveal What Kind of
   Classes They Like to See on a Résumé." *Back Stage*, April 14, 2011. http://www.back
   stage.com/bso/news-and-features-spotlights/training-to-stand-out-1005134182
   .story. Accessed June 13, 2011.

"Report: Earnings for WGA Screenwriters Fell 10% in 2010." *Los Angeles Times*, July 1,
   2011. [online] Accessed http://latimesblogs.latimes.com/entertainmentnewsbuzz/
   2011/07/wga-earnings-guild.html, July 6, 2011.

Robbins, Noah. "Broadway Bound: Meet the new Eugene Jerome, Neil Simon's alter ego
   in the Brighton Beach Memoirs revival. His Name Is Noah Robbins, He's 19, and He
   Just Moved to New York." *New York Magazine*, October 11, 2009. http://nymag.com/
   news/intelligencer/breaking/59905/. Accessed June 21, 2011.

Roe, Jonathan. "The Average Cost of a Bachelors Degree." eHow. http://www.ehow.com/
   about_5382752_average-cost-bachelors-degree.html. Accessed April 25, 2011.

Roundabout Theatre Company. "Education Brochure 2009–2010." http://content.yudu.
   com/Library/A1rpmy/EducationRoundabout2/resources/4.htm. Accessed April 25,
   2011.

Russell, Paul. *Acting: Make It Your Business.* New York: Back Stage Books, 2008.

Samberg, Joel. "30 Years On: Hostra's theatre class of '79 takes a look back." *Dramatics*,
   April 2010, pages 31–33, 44.

"School for prospective Billy Elliots." *Gifted and Talented Update*, September 2005. http://
   www.teachingexpertise.com/articles/school-prospective-billy-elliots-107. Accessed
   June 21, 2011.

Segal, David. "Is Law School a Losing Game?" *New York Times*, January 9, 2011, business
   section, 1, 6–7.

Steinberg, Jacques. "'Best Colleges'? Counselors Beg to Differ with U.S. News." *New
   York Times*, May 19, 2011. http://thechoice.blogs.nytimes.com/2011/05/19/nacac-on
   -usnews/June 20. Accessed 2011.

———. "Graduates Fault Advice of Guidance Counselors." *New York Times*, March 3,
   2010. http://www.nytimes.com/2010/03/03/education/03guidance.html. Accessed
   June 20, 2011.

———. "Plan B: Skip College." *New York Times*, May 16, 2010, B1.

Slotnick, Daniel E. and Richard Pérez-Peña. "College Says It Exaggerated SAT Figures for
   Ratings." *New York Times,* January 31, 2012, A12.

Smith, Alistair. "Cameron Mackintosh Closes in on Andrew Lloyd Webber in Sunday
   Times Rich List." http://www.thestage.co.uk/news/newsstory.php/27990/cameron

-mackintosh-closes-in-on-andrew-lloyd. Accessed April 25, 2011.

Smith, Sean. "The Summer Sequel We Don't Want to See." *Entertainment Weekly*, May 23, 2008. http://www.ew.com/ew/article/0,,20201915,00.html. Accessed July 9, 2011.

Stage Directors and Choreographers Society. "Membership Benefits." http://sdcweb.org/index.php?option=com_content&task=view &id=35&Itemid=91. Accessed April 25, 2011.

Theatre Communications Group website. http://www.tcg.org/index.cfm. Accessed April 25, 2011.

Theatre Development Fund website. http://www.tdf.org/

Topaz, Muriel, and Carole Everett. *Guide to Performing Arts Programs: Profiles of Over 600 Colleges, High Schools, and Summer Programs*. New York: Random House, 1998.

"2011 College and University Programs in Theater." *Back Stage*, March 2, 2011. http://www.backstage.com/bso/production-listings/2011-college-and-university-programs-in-1005057112.story. Accessed June 21, 2011.

U.S. Bureau of Labor Statistics. "2008–2018 Occupational Outlook." http://www.bls.gov/oco. Accessed April 2011.

U.S. Census Bureau. "American Community Survey." http://www.census.gov/acs/www/. Accessed April 20, 2011.

U.S. Department of Education. "Jacob K. Javits Fellowship Program Performance Assessment: 2000–01 Cohort Participant Results." http://www2.ed.gov/programs/jacob javits/performance.html. Accessed April 25, 2011.

———. "Higher Education Opportunity Act Information on College Costs" website. http://collegecost.ed.gov/. Accessed April 25, 2011.

United Scenic Artists website. http://www.usa829.org/. Accessed April 25, 2011.

University/Resident Theatre Association website. http://www.urta.com/. Accessed April 25, 2011.

University of California-Los Angeles. "About the Undergraduate Theater." http://www.tft.ucla.edu/programs/undergraduate-theater/about/. Accessed April 25, 2011.

Unwin, Stephen. *So You Want To Be a Theatre Director?* London: Nick Hern Books, 2004.

Volz, Jim. *The Back Stage Guide to Working in Regional Theater*. New York: Back Stage Books, 2007.

von Zastrow, Claus, and Helen Janc. "Academic Atrophy: The Condition of the Liberal Arts in America's Public Schools." Council for Basic Education, 2004. http://www.menc.org/documents/legislative/AcademicAtrophy.pdf. Accessed April 25, 2011.

Walters, Scott. "Mike Wiley: One's a Crowd." *American Theatre* 28 (April 2011): 42–44.

Weiner, David, and Jodie Langel. *Making It on Broadway: Actors' Tales of Climbing to the Top*. New York: Allworth Press, 2004.

Yankelovitch, Daniel, W. Norton Grubb, and Charles Murray. "Are Too Many Students Going to College?" *Chronicle of Higher Education*, November 13, 2009, B7–B10.

Zimmerman, Eilene. "Career Couch: Helping Teenagers Find Their Dreams." *New York Times*, October 25, 2009, business section, 8.

CPSIA information can be obtained at www.ICGtesting.com
Printed in the USA
LVOW090824130612

285918LV00002B/1/P

9 781611 170818